Kolin 1757

Frederick the Great's first defeat

OSPREY
PUBLISHING

Kolin 1757

Frederick the Great's first defeat

Simon Millar • Illustrated by Adam Hook

Series editor Lee Johnson • Consultant editor David G Chandler

First published in Great Britain in 2001 by Osprey Publishing, Elms Court, Chapel Way, Botley, Oxford OX2 9LP United Kingdom
Email: info@ospreypublishing.com

ISBN 1 84176 297 0

Editor: Lee Johnson
Design: Ken Vail Graphic Design, Cambridge, UK
Index by Alan Thatcher
Maps by The Map Studio
3D bird's eye views by John Plumer
Battlescene artwork by Adam Hook
Originated by Grasmere Digital Imaging, Leeds, UK
Printed in China through World Print Ltd.

00 01 02 03 04   10 9 8 7 6 5 4 3 2 1

For a catalogue of all books published by Osprey Military and Aviation please contact:

The Marketing Manager, Osprey Direct UK,
PO Box 140, Wellingborough,
Northants, NN8 4ZA, United Kingdom.
Email: info@ospreydirect.co.uk

The Marketing Manager, Osprey Direct USA,
c/o Motorbooks International, PO Box 1,
Osceola, WI 54020-0001, USA.
Email: info@ospreydirectusa.com

www.ospreypublishing.com

Dedication

To my eldest son Rupert, a battlefield companion.

Acknowledgements

In writing this book I have received considerable assistance from Phillip Haythornthwaite (PH), Wolfgang Friedrich in Dresden, Petr Klucina of the Czech Army Museum in Prague, Romain Baulesch in Vienna, Vladimír Delínek in Prague and Lucie Rysavá for her Czech translation skills; also my thanks to Gerhard Althaus of the Preussen Museum, Minden (PM), Dr Gerhard Bauer of the Militärhistorisches Museum der Bundeswehr, Dresden (MMB), HR Dr. Brigitte Holl of the Heeresgeschichtliches Museum, Vienna (HGM), Helmut Selzer of the Museum der Stadt, Wien (MSW), the staff of the Regional Museum, Kolin and Peter Harrington of the Anne SK Brown University Library, Rhode Island (ASKB).

Artist's Note

Readers may care to note that the original paintings from which the colour plates in this book were prepared are available for private sale. All reproduction copyright whatsoever is retained by the publisher. All enquiries should be addressed to:

Scorpio Gallery, PO Box 475, Hailsham,
East Sussex BN27 2SL UK

The publishers regret that they can enter into no correspondence on this matter.

KEY TO MILITARY SYMBOLS

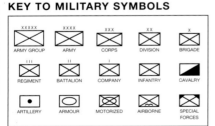

CONTENTS

THE RISE OF PRUSSIA AND THE ROAD TO WAR

THE POLITICAL BACKGROUND

The campaign of Kolin was fought in the second year of the Seven Years War. The first campaign of the war, Frederick's invasion of Saxony, began in the late summer of 1756. In the two and a half centuries since, the question of who started the war has been keenly debated. The period 1697–1740 was one of shifting alliances and political intrigue in Europe and witnessed the rise of Brandenburg-Prussia. The seeds of the Seven Years War were also sown at this time.

The creation of the army and administrative machinery that would dominate the development of Brandenburg-Prussia as a modern state, began during the reign of Frederick William (1640–88) 'The Great Elector'. By the end of the Thirty Years War a standing army had become an important symbol of state power and prestige, and a prerequisite of political influence. This was a lesson not lost on the Great Elector and by the time of his death in 1688 he had created an efficient, disciplined and unified force of 30,000 men out of European mercenaries and the indigenous population. He also bequeathed to his successor, Frederick III (1688–1713), a close allegiance to the Emperor, which was maintained, and the belief in a universal Christian Empire. A series of defensive alliances with Sweden, England and the Dutch placed Brandenburg-Prussia firmly in the anti-French camp. Fear of French expansionism kept Brandenburg-Prussia within this network for the duration of his reign. In 1692, Ernst Augustus of Brunswick-Hanover had been granted an electoral title, much to the chagrin of Frederick III, who had been seeking a royal title for many years. From this moment onwards his desire to be recognised as king coloured his relationship with Emperor Leopold I. In 1700 the royal courts of Europe were nervous over the succession to the Spanish Empire and to complicate matters the Bavarian Electoral prince, who was a potential heir to the Spanish Empire, died in 1699 casting even more doubt over the whole question of the succession. In 1697 the youthful Charles XII had succeeded to the Swedish throne. Augustus of Saxony-Poland, Christian IV of Denmark and Peter I of Russia wasted no time in plotting the demise of the young king and the dismemberment of the Swedish Empire. The Great Northern War (1700–21) began and for the time being Brandenburg-Prussia remained on the side lines. With his country's location on a key east-west axis, Frederick III realised he would play a pivotal role in any future developments in the region. To avoid interference in their planned carve-up of Swedish territory, the allied states of Saxony-Poland, Russia and Denmark were all willing to support Frederick in his quest for recognition of his royal title. The Emperor, Leopold I, was reluctant to oblige Frederick III, but events were about to play into Frederick's

Empress Maria Theresa, a steadfast opponent of Frederick II who was adored by her troops. (MSW)

7

hands. Leopold was angered when William III of England and Louis XIV of France proposed to partition the Spanish inheritance between the claimants. If war broke out, which seemed likely, Brandenburg-Prussia's military strength could be a valuable asset. Leopold decided to agree to Frederick's demands and recognised Frederick's claim to be King 'in Prussia'. In return Frederick was to supply the imperial armies with 8,000 men in the event of war and to support the Emperor's son and heir the Archduke Joseph as Holy Roman Emperor, when the time came. Frederick was crowned in Königsberg in January 1701, as Frederick I of Prussia. His coronation marked the culmination of the Hohenzollern quest for recognition as a European royal dynasty, and the coming of age of Brandenburg-Prussia as a state. Two days after the coronation, the King of Spain died and Prussia was embroiled in the War of the Spanish Succession. Frederick managed to avoid being dragged into the Great Northern War against Sweden and his neutrality and passivity had lost him nothing, but the turmoil in Europe confirmed to him the need for a powerful army to defend the borders of Prussia against her large and often predatory neighbours.

In 1713 Frederick I died and his son Frederick William came to the throne. He inherited a small but professional army, 40,000 strong, that had fought with distinction in the War of the Spanish Succession. Frederick William carried on his fathers programme of building up the army and was particularly dedicated to his guardsmen, above all the Potsdam Grenadiers, famous for being exceptionally tall soldiers. Frederick William even took to wearing military uniform at court, so did his courtiers, as a matter of routine. This symbolised not only to his people but also the foreign ambassadors the pre-eminent position of the army in Prussian affairs. By the time of his death in 1740, 1 in 25 subjects were serving in the army and Frederick William had raised state expenditure on the army from 50 per cent under his father to 80 per cent. The Prussian army stood at 80,000 well-trained and disciplined men. In many respects the army did not exist to serve the state; quite the opposite, Brandenburg-Prussia existed to serve the army. This extraordinary state of affairs was going to have serious political and economic consequences.

In 1740 Frederick William I of Prussia and the Emperor Charles VI died within five months of each other. Frederick II (1712–1788), later to be called 'the Great' succeeded his father and was to be the benefactor of his forebear's foresight for he now had a formidable army at his disposal.

During his banishment from his father's court after the aborted escape attempt with the unfortunate Katte (see p.18), Frederick was tutored by Christoph Werner Hille. Hille taught Frederick the importance of the River Oder and how vital it was for Prussia to acquire Silesia. Frederick very quickly learnt the litany – What is the Oder? The Oder is the only important river flowing through Brandenburg-Prussian territory. And Stettin? The port at the mouth of the Oder and must always be seen as the natural harbour for Berlin. Silesia? If Brandenburg-Prussia controls Silesia, the river Oder is controlled and so is the Oder trade. Frederick had clearly realised that the rich Habsburg province of Silesia was vital to the prosperity of Prussia. Maria Theresa, who succeeded her father as Empress and Queen of Hungary, came into possession of the vast, rambling and run-down Habsburg domains, known as the Holy Roman Empire. The Pragmatic Sanction of 1713, drawn up by her father, Charles VI, aimed to ensure European recognition of the indivisibility of Habsburg lands and the right of a female to inherit. Charles though had one specific female in mind, his daughter, Maria Theresa, who took precedence over the daughters of his dead brother, the Emperor Joseph I. The Pragmatic Sanction therefore arbitrarily disinherited one of his nieces, who was married to Charles Albert, Elector of Bavaria.

Maria Theresa was a determined woman, and Frederick realised that he was not going to win Silesia by diplomatic means. Under the circumstances he was quite happy to resort to force of arms. Without waiting to confirm his legal position, Frederick used some tenuous Prussian claims to the duchies of Liegnitz, Brieg and Wolhau in the Silesian lands to justify his invasion on 16 December 1740 at the head of 24,000 troops. 'With flags waving and music sounding, I have crossed the Rubicon,' so Frederick wrote to his minister Podewils. Frederick had certainly crossed the Rubicon, he was engaged in the first of two Silesian Wars, sometimes known as the War of the Austrian Succession (1740–42 and 1744–45) and with his victories at Mollwitz, Chotusitz, Hohenfriedberg and Soor, he would find himself in a position of pre-eminence as a King-Commander at the end of the wars. At the Peace of Dresden, signed on Christmas Day 1745, Maria Theresa recognised his sovereignty over Silesia and the Duchy of Glatz. All she gained in return was Frederick's agreement to support the election of her consort Francis Stephen as Emperor of Germany.

Maria Theresa believed wholeheartedly in the Pragmatic Sanction's declaration of the unity of the Habsburg lands and saw it as her duty to defend this inheritance. As a result she would never allow the Peace of Dresden to stand in the long term. However, it bought her time to consolidate her position as Empress, reorganise her crippled army and make new alliances. Her sole intention was to regain Silesia, thereby restoring the Pragmatic Sanction and her borders to those of 1740. Her aim was also to reduce Brandenburg-Prussia, Austria's implacable enemy, to the status of a minor European state. The seeds of the Seven Years War were thus sown in Austria's defeat in the Silesian Wars.

There was a period between the Silesian Wars and the start of the Seven Years War that has become known as 'The Diplomatic Revolution'. In 1750 Maria Theresa began to turn for advice to a young member of her Cabinet, Anton Wenzel von Kaunitz who would shortly become the arbiter of Austria's foreign policy for upward of 40 years. Kaunitz believed that the strongest alliance against the Prussian king would be formed by those states who felt threatened by Prussian expansion. Diplomatic manoeuvring to create the right 'conditions' for a lasting treaty began to bear fruit in 1756. The key was the changing relationship between Vienna and Paris. Since 1740 the French had been in uneasy alliance with Prussia, a relationship severely tested by Frederick's ambiguous foreign policies. The treaty was due to expire in 1756. The only benefit France could see from continuing with the treaty was the possibility that Prussia might invade Hanover and in so doing reduce the pressure on France in her struggle with England (Britain was not a term commonly used at this time) in North America, India and on the high seas. The strongest argument against her treaty with Prussia, however, was France's need to break up the traditional alliance between Austria

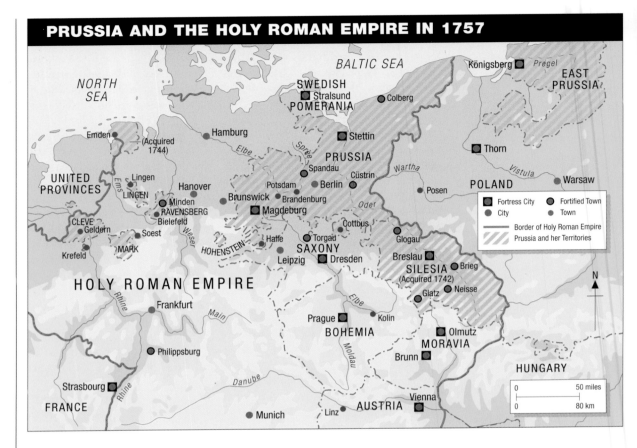

and England. With this in mind France proved receptive to Austrian diplomatic overtures. Austria sought an ally in her struggle against Prussia and the French hoped to prevent Austria entering any war on the side of England. On 16 January 1756 England and Prussia signed the Convention of Westminster, by which both states agreed not to allow foreign troops of any nation to pass through or enter Germany. England, to protect Hanover, had secured the services of 55,000 Russian troops in the subsidy treaty of St. Petersburg in 1755, but she no longer wished to use these on German soil. Frederick agreed to defend Hanover, if the Electorate was attacked by France. Both powers 'guaranteed the neutrality of Germany', but specifically excluded the Austrian Netherlands. Prussia was recognised as England's strongest ally on the Continent. Having converted one enemy into an ally and rid himself of another – Russia – Frederick had preserved the neutrality of Germany and simultaneously excluded Russian and French troops. The effect of this treaty was immediate and enormous. In St. Petersburg Elizabeth, who hated Frederick with a passion, declared the subsidy treaty of 1755 with England to be dead. This is hardly surprising when one considers the attitude to Frederick of Elizabeth and the Russian Council, which in October 1755 had solemnly declared that Russia would aid any power which attacked Prussia. Negotiations between France and Austria concluded satisfactorily on 1 May 1756 with the signing of the Treaty of Versailles – the alliance was sealed. The alliance actually consisted of three separate treaties – two public and one secret. The first was an act of neutrality by Austria; she agreed to take no part in hostilities between England and France. France for her part undertook not to invade the Austrian Netherlands or any other Austrian possession. The second treaty was by nature a defensive alliance and a treaty of friendship, whereby each power agreed to defend the possessions of the other if attacked – the existing war against France and England being excepted. The third treaty, of five secret articles, included the agreement that Austria would aid France if attacked by an ally of England. Neither power was able to make any new alliances without mutual agreement. In January 1757 Russia, on hearing of the treaty, passed the convention of St. Petersburg, recognising the defensive alliance between Austria and France. A new Treaty of Versailles was signed on 1 May 1757 and in this treaty, France agreed to the partition of Prussia and undertook to pay Austria an annual subsidy to place a strong army in the field. In return France was to receive a portion of the Netherlands. These two treaties created two new camps in European affairs. France and Austria, aided by the expansionist Russian nation; and that of England and Prussia, two new and very ambitious Powers. The 'Diplomatic Revolution' had come to an end.

FREDERICK'S INVASION OF SAXONY

Frederick had been made aware, by his spies in The Hague, that the armies of his enemies were deploying to invade Brandenburg-Prussia. He reasoned that by moving first he would not only surprise his enemies and hopefully put them out of their stride, but that by attacking Saxony he could knock her out of the war and prevent her providing manpower for the Austrian armies. He would gain a useful base for operations in Bohemia and a vital buffer zone between Habsburg lands and Brandenburg-Prussia, thus avoiding the war being fought on Prussian territory. The first campaign of the Seven Years War began on 29 August 1756 when Frederick and 62,000 men invaded Saxony. He led the main army towards Dresden himself, while Prince Ferdinand of Brunswick led the right wing towards Leipzig.

Frederick found Dresden undefended and on 9 September he entered the Saxon capital. The Saxon army had withdrawn, with no great urgency, down the left (west) bank of the River Elbe towards their Austrian allies. Frederick encountered the Saxon army on 10 September, entrenched in a strong position that was to become known as the Camp of Pirna. The Saxon camp while formidable made the Austrian task of helping them even more difficult. The Saxons would pay for their lethargy. Neither side wanted to fire the first shot and be seen as the aggressor and so Frederick, with his army, settled down to wait for the Saxons to surrender. On 13 September Frederick pushed his troops over the border into Bohemia partly in search of fresh forage and partly to reassure himself as to the location of the Austrian army. Field Marshal Maximillian Ulysses von Browne, a very capable Austrian commander, had been tasked with rescuing the 15,000 strong Saxon army. His force was concentrating in northern Bohemia. Browne had a bold plan to send a corps from Bohemia across the mountainous border on the right (east) bank of the Elbe into Saxony. The Saxons would then cross the

Elbe and retreat with the Austrians back into Bohemia. Frederick, however, was frustrating these plans by feeding more and more troops into northern Bohemia and Browne had to deal with this problem first. Frederick, sceptical of the accuracy of the reports he was receiving from Field Marshal Keith about Browne's movements, assumed personal command of his army in Bohemia on 28 September. Within two days Frederick had led his small army of 29,000 men over the Mittel-Gebirge to Wellemin. Browne, needing to deal with Frederick before he could rescue the Saxons, encountered the Prussians at Lobositz on 1 October 1756. The battle was hard fought and Frederick, just as at Mollwitz, thought the battle was lost and was leaving the field when he sent a final order to Bevern to try one more attack. The attack was successful and by 4.00pm the Austrians had withdrawn from the field. The tactical victory had gone to the Prussians, but the Austrians were not routed and still posed a genuine threat to Frederick. The Prussians had met a very different enemy this time and many a veteran of the Silesian wars muttered, 'these are no longer the old Austrians'. Although he had failed to defeat Frederick, Browne's plan remained intact; he took command of the relieving force himself and marched to rescue the Saxons. Although the Saxons crossed the Elbe as planned they were unable to make contact with Browne and demoralised and badly led they surrendered to the Prussians on 13 October. Browne decided that by sealing off the countryside with his Croats and making life intolerable for the Prussians he could force them to evacuate Bohemia. He achieved this aim admirably and by the end of October the Prussians were in full retreat back into Saxony.

CHRONOLOGY

1640–88 The reign of Frederick William, 'The Great Elector'

1700–21 The Great Northern War

1701–14 War of the Spanish Succession

1701 **January** – Elector Frederick III is crowned as King Frederick I of Prussia at Königsberg

1713–40 Reign of Frederick William, Frederick the Great's father. He greatly expands the army

1713 The Pragmatic Sanction. Emperor Charles VI, with no male children, attempts to ensure the succession of his daughter Maria Theresa

1740–86 Reign of Frederick II, 'The Great'

1740 **20 October** – Death of Emperor Charles VI

1740–80 Reign of Maria Theresa

1740–48 Wars of the Austrian Succession

1740–42 First Silesian War

1741 **10 April** – Battle of Mollwitz

1742 **17 May** – Battle of Chotusitz

1744–45 Second Silesian War

1745 **4 June** – Battle of Hohenfriedberg

30 September – Battle of Soor

14 December – Battle of Kesselsdorf

25 December – Peace of Dresden. Maria Theresa recognises Frederick's sovereignty over Silesia

1756–63 The Seven Years War

1756 **16 January** – England and Prussia sign the Convention of Westminster. Both states agree not to allow foreign troops of any nation to enter or pass through Germany

1 May – France and Austria sign the Treaty of Versailles

29 August – Frederick invades Saxony

9 September – The Prussians occupy the Saxon capital, Dresden

10 September – Frederick begins the 'siege' of the Saxon camp at Pirna

1 October – Battle of Lobositz. Frederick wins a hard-fought victory. The performance of the Austrians leads some Prussian veterans to comment that 'these are no longer the old Austrians'

13 October – Saxons surrender to Frederick

1757 **January** – Convention of St. Petersburg. Russia recognises the defensive alliance between Austria and Russia

18 April – Frederick begins his invasion of Bohemia

21 April – Battle of Reichenberg

1 May – In a new Treaty of Versailles France agrees to the partition of Prussia and to pay the Austrians a subsidy to keep a strong army in the field. In return France is to receive a portion of the Netherlands

6 May – Battle of Prague. Frederick defeats the Austrian army in another hard-fought battle, forcing the bulk of the army back into Prague

29 May – The bombardment of Prague begins

18 June – Battle of Kolin. Frederick's defeat forces him to abandon the siege of Prague and retreat into Saxony

OPPOSING COMMANDERS

THE AUSTRIANS

The Austrian army that took the field in the Seven Years War had undergone a major reorganisation after the Silesian Wars. The more ineffectual commanders had made way for a younger and in most cases a more able officer.

Maria Theresa, Empress of the Holy Roman Empire and Queen of Hungary (1717–1780)

Although Maria Theresa did not command in the field personally, she conscientiously exercised her position as the Commander-in-Chief of her armies, taking a very close interest in the affairs and campaigns of the army that fought under her colours. Maria Theresa was married to Francis Stephen of Lorraine, who was a charming but ineffectual man. Maria Theresa was 23 when she became Empress of the Holy Roman Empire and Queen of Hungary. She was beautiful, kind and trusted her fellow monarchs. She was in for a rude shock, for within months she was at war with half of Europe. She was hindered in defending the Empire by both senile and short-sighted advisors at court, and an army the remnants of which were demoralised after disastrous campaigns against the Turks. To cap it all the state was virtually bankrupt and her people disaffected. Through her charm, courage and resolute will she succeeded in holding her enemies at bay. Although her armies had been defeated time and again, most particularly by Frederick II of Prussia in the Silesian Wars, the state had survived and she seized her chance to reorganise and revitalise it.

Between the two major wars of her reign, she chose new advisors and instituted reforms to unify the disparate lands and peoples of the Empire. Field Marshal Leopold Graf Daun and Field Marshal Joseph Wenzel Prince Liechtenstein were appointed to reform the infantry and artillery respectively after the poor performance in the Silesian Wars. Under Maria Theresa loyalty to the crown, herself in particular, was far more important than one's place of birth. She would watch the columns as they marched through Vienna on their way to the wars; they were her children and she knew that by taking a personal

Wenzel Anton Graf Kaunitz-Rietberg, an Austrian by birth. He joined the Imperial Court Council at 24 in 1735 and then entered the diplomatic service. By 1749 he had impressed Maria Theresa and was set to become the most powerful and brilliant of her advisors. (MSW)

interest in their affairs she would gain their respect. She received in return far more than that – her soldiers loved her deeply and the more they saw of her resolute courage and steadfastness the more this affection grew. In 1754, while her husband the Emperor Francis Stephen went hunting, Maria Theresa was inspecting the Grand Manoeuvres in Bohemia. Over the years she gained enormous insight into the affairs of the army and on more than one occasion put her generals to shame with her depth of knowledge. She took enormous pride in the belief that the army went about their business with confidence in their ability and the knowledge that they had been tested in battle, rather than with the starched discipline of the Prussians. For Maria Theresa her wars against Prussia were for the survival of her Catholic empire against a nation of heretics, led by a Godless king.

Field Marshal Leopold Graf von Daun (1705–1766)

Leopold Daun was born on 27 September 1705, the son of Field Marshal Wirich von Daun. In 1718 at the age of 13 he entered the army of Emperor Leopold I as an ensign. At the age of 26 Daun was promoted to Colonel and was appointed to command the infantry regiment of which his father was the *Inhaber* or colonel proprietor. At the end of the Polish war of Succession in 1736 Daun was promoted to Major-General. He fought in the numerous campaigns Austria waged unsuccessfully against the Ottoman Empire at this time. A year into the first Silesian War, Daun became the *Inhaber* of his own regiment and at the battle of Chotusitz (17 May 1742) established a reputation for coolness under fire. In 1745 at the age of 40 he married Josepha Gräffin von Füchs, the widow of Field Marshal Nostitz and in the same year their daughter Maria Theresa was born. In 1745 after the battles of Hohenfriedberg and Soor he became the armaments minister. The first years after the Peace of Dresden were quiet for Daun and between 1746 and 1748 his two sons Franz Karl and Leopold were born. He was one of the major reformers of the Austrian military system. Between the wars he wrote the new regulations for infantry and cavalry training and became head of the Army Academy in Vienna. Daun was promoted to Field Marshal in 1756. After the battle of Leuthen in 1757 he became overall Commander-in-Chief in the field. After his victory at Kolin, he defeated the Prussians at Hochkirch and Maxen, but lost at Liegnitz and Torgau. Daun was always looking to improve the staff work within the Austrian army and in 1758 he gained Maria Theresa's consent to establish a proper general staff. In 1759 Daun commissioned the first horse artillery battery in the Austrian army, and he was a champion of the engineer corps. When the Austrians captured a copy of Frederick's *Military Instructions for his Generals*, Daun was so impressed with them he wrote a memorandum for the Imperial circle. Daun was

Field Marshal Leopold Graf von Daun, lauded as the man who gave Maria Theresa her first victory over Frederick. An able, but cautious commander who won victories at Hochkirch (1758) and Maxen (1759) but was beaten at Torgau (1760). It was his reforms to the infantry that made them a far more formidable opponent to Frederick than the Prussian monarch expected. (ASKB)

an able commander, his greatest strengths were his organisational skills and his grasp of logistics, his ability to manoeuvre effectively, and a good eye for ground. He was a true professional and paid particular attention to inspections at the front and to camp security. When it came to exploiting a victory or taking the offensive, however, he left much to be desired. Frederick caused the majority of his opponents to err on the side of timidity and being a naturally cautious man, at times Daun was not able to differentiate between prudent caution and straightforward vacillation. Nevertheless, Daun will always be remembered as the commander who gave the Austrians their first victory over Frederick. Maria Theresa instituted the Order of Maria Theresa in celebration of his victory at Kolin.

General Franz Leopold Graf Nadasty (1708–1783)

General Franz Leopold Nadasty was a Hungarian officer and nobleman. He was a true light cavalry officer – brave, selfless, enterprising and lively. The whole of the Austrian mounted arm was devoted to him and even the infantry held him in high esteem. He first made his name leading his Hussars during the Silesian Wars. His raids were daring, his reconnaissance always thorough with every likelihood that he would launch a lightning attack. It was at Soor (30 September 1745) that having undertaken a careful reconnaissance of the Prussian right flank, Nadasty found that the Austrians could make a concealed attack on the Prussian right. During the battle Nadasty also came across a convoy with the Prussian royal baggage and in true Hussar spirit plundered Frederick's tents, horses, money chest, table silver and clothes. Biche, Frederick's favourite whippet, was also taken but was in time returned to him. When he was tasked with commanding the siege at Schweidnitz, the static nature of the warfare and slow momentum frustrated him greatly. He eventually ran out of patience and ordered an assault which to his joy was successful. Leuthen was his last field command. After the débâcle he was retired to satisfy the Lorraine faction at court. Nadasty received his Order of Maria Theresa on 7 March 1758.

Johann Baptist Graf Serbelloni

Serbelloni was born into the Lombard aristocracy. He was an aloof individual and as such came across as a cold man. When called to the colours on mobilisation in September 1756 he reported to Piccolomini's headquarters and made the presumptuous remark, 'the Empress should not be under the illusion that she can order about a General of Cavalry like a major'. In many respects Serbelloni was a typical aristocratic officer of his time, he stood 'on his rank' and enjoyed the creature comforts of home. In 1760 when many of the incompetent commanders were retired, Serbelloni was able to survive due to his connections at court. In an army where German was the language of command he was notoriously inept at speaking the language, and frequently became annoyed when aides repeated messages thinking he might not have understood. When given independent command he was lethargic, almost idle. He offered no resistance to the Prussians during the spring invasion of Bohemia in 1757 and withdrew towards Prague. The handling of his command was so pedestrian that on the day of the Battle of Prague he was still some miles from the field and made no attempt to march to the sound of the guns. On occasion and when under command of a senior officer he was a brave and reliable commander, leading his cavalry with a certain amount of dash.

THE PRUSSIANS

Unlike the Austrians, the Prussians had the successes of the Silesian Wars behind them. Therefore, unless too old for active service, the majority of commanders, were at the front again in the Seven Years War.

Frederick II, King of Prussia and Elector of Brandenburg (1712–1786)

Frederick in some respects was an ambiguous man, on the one hand he was the 'Philosopher-Prince', a friend of Voltaire, and on the other a Spartan, militaristic King with simple tastes. Frederick was born in 1712 and was 28 when he became King in 1740. Growing up at court, where he suffered often quite brutal treatment at the hands of his father, Frederick William I, Frederick gave no indication of an interest in the military profession. He was intelligent and slight, only 5ft 7ins as an adult, who much preferred being left to his own devices; reading and playing the flute. In 1730 Frederick and his close friend Hermann von Katte tried to

Frederick II, King of Prussia, called 'the Great'. A likeness of Frederick in about 1770. Frederick was hardly ever seen out of his uniform of a plain blue coat with the Order of the Black Eagle on his left breast. (Engraving after Madel)

escape his father's court. At the age of 14 Frederick had been commissioned in the Potsdam Grenadiers. Von Katte was a young officer in the Gendarmes, as such Frederick William I viewed their escapade as desertion. Both were arrested and imprisoned and tried by Court Martial. The court sentenced von Katte to life imprisonment, but could not pass judgment on Frederick – as the Crown Prince only the King could decide his fate. Frederick William changed von Katte's sentence to death and Frederick was to be exiled within the kingdom. Firstly, however, Frederick was forced to watch the execution of his friend. He was then banished to the fortress of Küstrin. Here he learnt about local government, industry, trade and agriculture. Eventually Frederick and his father were reconciled and both realised that as long as they lived apart they would get on. In 1732 Frederick was given the Colonelcy of the Goltz Regiment of Foot and in the same year he married Elizabeth Christina of Brunswick-Wolfenbüttel. In 1736 Frederick moved to the castle at Rheinsberg, which was perfectly placed, close to the two garrison towns of his regiment at Neu-Ruppin and Naun. Whilst at Rheinsberg Frederick gathered around him his own small circle of trusted advisors. One of these was Kurt Christoph von Schwerin. A firm but enlightened disciplinarian, Schwerin had an enormous influence on Frederick and it was during this time that Frederick came to the conclusion that he would be a soldier-king. He was at Rheinsberg when his father died in 1740 and within a few months Frederick had plunged Europe into war. He took advantage of Maria Theresa's recent accession to the throne in Austria to invade Silesia. The Silesian Wars, with Prussian victories at Mollwitz (1741), Chotusitz (1742), Hohenfriedberg (1745) and Soor (1745) saw the start of Prussian military ascendancy over Austria. In many respects Frederick was without moral scruple and would wage war if this course of action suited his policy. When in 1740 his minister of state, Podewills, suggested politely that his claim to certain duchies in Silesia was debatable and that his reason therefore for making war on Maria Theresa was dubious he answered, 'when one has the advantage, should one not make use of it?'

General Moritz Fürst von Anhalt-Dessau (1712–1760)

Born in 1712 Moritz of Anhalt-Dessau was the youngest son of Leopold of Anhalt-Dessau, the famous 'Alte Dessauer'. Moritz is said to have had no education at all – an experiment by his father. Considered illiterate by his contemporaries he was able to read and understand letters and write in a simple style. He did however inherit from his father a natural talent for soldiering. He earned the Order of the Black Eagle on the field of Kesseldorf (1745) and was promoted to Field Marshal at Leuthen. Moritz was not suitable for independent command, unless surrounded by a very capable staff. He was undoubtedly a brave man but with little imagination. At Zorndorf in 1758 Frederick exclaimed 'May God have mercy on our souls'. The dogged Moritz, determined to win the day, threw his hat in the air and shouted 'Long live the King!

Having had no formal education General of Infantry Moritz Fürst von Anhalt-Dessau, the youngest son of 'The Old Dessauer', was not blessed with a great intellect. He was however a steadfast and determined commander, but never given an independent command by Frederick. He was Frederick's nominated second-in-command at Kolin. (ASKB)

Lieutenant-General Augustus Wilhelm Herzog zu Braunschweig-Luneburg (Bevern), a cousin of Ferdinand of Brunswick he was a reliable commander well liked by his peers and men. He fell out of favour for a while when Frederick was of the opinion that he let himself be captured after failing at Breslau in 1757. (ASKB)

We've won the battle' and promptly led Dohna's infantry into the attack. The advance did not last long, 36 squadrons of Russian cavalry thundered down on the isolated attack and threw it back. Wounded at the Battle of Hochkirch (1758) he died of his wounds without returning to the army.

Lieutenant-General August Wilhelm Herzog zu Braunschweig-Luneburg (Bevern) (1715–1781)

Bevern was a rare breed amongst officers of his day, even in Frederick's army. He paid for professors to give classes to his young officers on mathematics and geometry. He even engaged 'foreign' private soldiers to hold classes in their native tongue. He was a brave and reliable commander who very rarely let Frederick down. It was Bevern who launched the last attack at Lobositz, pushing the Austrians off the Lobosch and winning the day for Frederick. Throughout his career he was trusted with independent command. He did however lose Frederick's confidence when his entrenched camp outside Breslau was stormed by the Austrians, and Bevern retreated over the River Oder. Breslau, the fortress capital of Silesia, fell to the Austrians on 25 November 1757. This was a fearful blow to Frederick and Bevern, quite rightly fearing the Royal wrath, allowed himself to be captured whilst on a reconnaissance. After he was exchanged he was sent to oversee the naval defence of Stettin and the Oder estuary. Frederick put great store by the need to defend Stettin, but for Bevern this was not a particularly exciting command and so over the winter of 1758/59 he oversaw the converting of local craft into warships. Deciding to strike at the nearest enemy he fought the Swedes at the action at Neuwarp, lost the battle and all but three of his ships. He re-built the flotilla to 12 vessels, but by 1762 he had once again been given a field command. Andrew Mitchell, the English envoy to Frederick, wrote, 'he [Bevern] was a worthy man, a great officer and beloved by the whole army'.

General Hans Joachim von Zieten (1699–1786)

Zieten was born in Wustrau in Brandenburg. His family, although landowners and members of the 'gentry' were poor and in many respects the classic Prussian 'Junker' that provided the core of Prussian regimental officers. Zieten was not a soldier who found life in barracks easy. His voice was not strong and he was a slight man who found it difficult to maintain discipline. He enjoyed his drink and when under its influence became sensitive and quarrelsome. This led him into two duels, a period of fortress arrest and even a temporary cashiering. On campaign however the true Zieten showed his colours. In 1740 at the start of the Silesian Wars Zieten was 42 and still a Lieutenant-Colonel of Hussars. He was an energetic commander who led the advance into Bohemia in 1744, and at Hohenfriedberg in 1745 it was Zieten who found a way across the Striegaur-Wasser and saved the Prussian cuirassiers in that sector from disaster. He led his cavalry with élan at Prague in 1757 and did all that was asked of him at Kolin. Later in the same year Zieten was sent to bring back the demoralised troops of Bevern's command, after the débâcle at Breslau in the days before Leuthen. Unlike many commanders who fail to live up to expectation when given independent command, Zieten at Torgau was Frederick's saviour. He was responsible for the improvements in quality and professionalism of the Prussian light cavalry.

COMMAND AND CONTROL IN THE EIGHTEENTH CENTURY

The 'Age of Reason' as the eighteenth century has come to be called, saw the rise of the professional officer class, primarily in the technical disciplines of the engineers and artillery and on the staff. Command and control of large armies in battle during this period presented commanders with significant problems. To help ease these problems commanders devolved command by appointing lower-ranking generals to lead elements of the army. To ease communication on the battlefield, as well as away from it, the commander appointed aides-de-camp to his suite. The positions were normally grace and favour. These young, well-connected officers had many reasons for accepting the duties of an ADC – some wished to escape the discipline of regimental soldiering, whilst others were dedicated followers of the commander they served. Both hoped for advancement. During this period however we also see a second group of officers at a commander's headquarters – the staff officer. Staff officers were a new breed of officer whose duties at first required them to tour the towns and villages selecting suitable 'quarters' for the senior officers and their staff; hence the name of their department, that of the Quartermaster General. Slowly but surely this department took over selecting the location of camps, the order of march and route selection. There were three other branches of the staff: the General Intendant, responsible for supply of food, ammunition and clothing; the Paymaster General who was, as his title suggests responsible for all the financial disbursements made by the army; and the Adjutant General, who along with his staff was responsible for keeping up to date the lists detailing the strength of the various regiments in the army, issuing orders, particularly those for battle, and compiling casualty returns. His department was also responsible for the orders detailing discipline and the arrangements for a Court Martial. Both the Austrians and the Prussians had departments who were responsible for procuring suitable guides. The Prussians had the *Capitaine des Guides* and the Austrians the *Wegemeister*. Maps were not particularly accurate – the majority being drawn with pencil or pen – and any variation in height had to be drawn on as maps lacked contours as we understand them. When the army moved through new territory the staff made an intensive study and notes were made for future reference.

Frederick had a great advantage over his enemies. As the King he was the ultimate authority for the direction of the campaigns for his army and unlike all the other monarchs of the period he was personally leading his men. The last British king to lead in battle personally was

General of Cavalry Hans Joachim von Zieten, a soldier who thrived on campaign and was responsible for the rise in the efficiency of the Prussian light cavalry. (ASKB)

RIGHT **Major-General Johann Dietrich von Hülsen (1693–1767). Promotion was slow for Hülsen, he was 51 when appointed to command Infantry Regiment No.36 (Munchow Fusiliers). Promoted to Major-General 9 September 1754 and awarded the Pour le Merite, 11 September 1754. A doughty commander who fought at Lobositz, Kolin, he was wounded at Kunersdorf (1759) and at Torgau (1760). Promoted to Lieutenant-General in 1758, he received the Order of the Black Eagle in the same year. Governor of Berlin in 1763. He died in 1767 and is buried in the Garrison Church, Potsdam. (ASKB)**

FAR RIGHT **Lieutenant-General Joachim Friedrich Christian von Tresckow (1698–1762). He started his military service in Infantry Regiment No. 6 (Guard Grenadier Battalion) in 1715. In 1737 Tresckow entered Russian service as a Captain in the Preobrajenski Guard Regiment. He fought in the 1739 campaign against the Turks as a Lieutenant-Colonel commanding a regiment. He was back in Prussian service in 1743. He fought at Soor (1745) and Kesselsdorf (1745) commanding a grenadier battalion. He was promoted to Lieutenant-General on 11 May 1757 and awarded the Order of the Black Eagle in the same year. Tresckow died in 1762. (ASKB)**

George II at the Battle of Dettingen in 1743. Maria Theresa, like her close ally Elizabeth of Russia, had to delegate the management of the campaigns to trusted and, she hoped, capable Generals. The Austrian commanders did enjoy operational freedom as a result of Maria Theresa's trust. Operational failures therefore were as a result of timidity or incompetence on the part of the commander, rather than a fault of the system or the fighting ability of the Austrian soldier.

No matter how many staff officers or advisors at a headquarters, the decision to give battle rests squarely on the shoulders of the commander. The decision to give battle in the eighteenth century normally resulted when manoeuvre had failed or a particular reason to engage existed. At Kolin Daun needed to relieve Prague – equally Frederick had to stop him. Plans for battle were issued to armies in an elaborate written form. The most complicated aspect of the plan was the order of march on to the battlefield, so that the correct tactical formation could be taken up. This procedure was complicated by the requirement to adhere to the seniority of the generals, some of whom were notoriously sensitive about this issue. Some commanders, most notably Frederick, also liked to give last minute briefings, particularly after a final reconnaissance. This could change the deployment for the battle and perhaps cause delay if any of the subsequent changes had to be written down. The commander could also make any changes necessary whilst the army was on the march and risk any resultant confusion.

Once battle had been joined the commander could in reality exercise limited control. He had to rely on the ability of his Generals to understand and carry out his orders and on the leadership abilities of his regimental officers. Commanders and the soldiers under them all suffered from the same factors affecting their performance – loyalty, religion, discipline, leadership and fear kept the soldier from running away, whereas the noise of battle, hunger, thirst, failure of discipline, casualties and fear all undermined his confidence.

OPPOSING ARMIES

I do not propose to dwell on the uniforms, tactical formations used by the infantry, cavalry or artillery or the various types of troops available to commanders. The Osprey Men-at-Arms volumes covering the Prussian Army and the Austrian Army by Philip Haythornthwaite give an excellent introduction to this subject.

The two armies that fought in the first campaign of 1757 were the result of very different backgrounds. The Prussian Army inherited by Frederick in 1740 numbered 83,000 men. The structure of his army had been established by his grandfather, Frederick I and developed by his father, Frederick William I. His father was a very military-minded monarch who took an enormous interest in the army, wearing uniform and acquiring the reputation of a drill sergeant in his attitudes and dealings with the army and his family. The result was that the Prussian Army was drilled to perfection. Frederick William was an eccentric, famous not only for his giant Potsdam Grenadiers but also for swapping a priceless porcelain collection for a fully equipped regiment of dragoons (Prussian Dragoon Regiment No. 6) from the Elector of Saxony in 1717. He treated his army like his own toy soldiers – they were not exposed to the rigours and dangers of war. This situation was to change dramatically when Frederick II came to the throne. Within the space of five years he had fought two wars, the first from 1740–42 to conquer Silesia and the second, 1744–45, to consolidate his conquest. Although the first battle between Frederick and his perennial foes the Austrians went in his favour, the Battle of Mollwitz (10 April 1741) was in many respects a 'near run thing'. The Prussian cavalry did not perform well, being soundly beaten and fleeing the field. Frederick left the battle early thinking he was defeated, only to be told later that his infantry had performed heroically and won the day for him. This pattern of the cavalry under-achieving and the infantry proving themselves to be in 'good order' continued at Chotusitz (17 May 1742); however, Frederick noted that the cavalry had performed better than at Mollwitz. Between the two wars Frederick produced a new *Reglement* each for the infantry, cavalry and artillery. He also wrote the *Seelowitz Instruction* (1742), which saw the beginnings of the 'Oblique Order'. During the second of the

Infantry Regiment No.35 (Prince Henry of Prussia). Garrison – Potsdam. One of Frederick's favoured regiments. This Fusilier regiment was in heavy fighting at Kolin (1757) and Kunersdorf (1759) where, in both battles, it won a high reputation. (Print after Knotel)

ABOVE LEFT **Fusilier of IR41 (Wied). Garrison – Minden. Another fusilier regiment that Frederick rated very highly. The regiment fought at Kolin, Kunersdorf (1759), Liegnitz (1760) and Torgau (1760). At Kolin the regiment suffered heavily losing nearly 70% casualties. (PM)**

ABOVE CENTRE **An officer of IR41 (Wied). This mannequin, along with the others, is part of a collection in the Preussen Museum in Minden, Nordrhein-Westphalen, Germany. (PM)**

ABOVE RIGHT **A mannequin of an NCO of IR41 (Wied). The indications of rank can be clearly seen – the gold lace on the cuff and the cane being carried in the right hand. Gauntlet-type gloves were also worn by NCOs. (PM)**

Silesian Wars Frederick saw a vast improvement in the abilities of his cavalry and artillery. The performance of the infantry and cavalry at the Battles of Hohenfriedberg (4 June 1745) and Soor (30 September 1745) showed the Prussians to be more than a match for the Austrians and their allies and that his *Reglements* of 1743 had been assimilated. Frederick put his success at Soor down to the 'most brave, the most valiant army that has existed'. The Prussian army was now amongst the foremost in Europe and Frederick had enormous confidence in himself and the abilities of his men. He was a copious writer and issued numerous sets of instructions to his troops. The most important being the *Principes Generaux de la Guerre* (1748), translated into German in the same year as the *General Principia vom Kriege*. These instructions eventually issued to his generals in 1753 as *The King of Prussia's Military Instructions for his Generals*, covered a range of subjects, from the faults and merits of the Prussian Army, the requirement for knowledge of the country his armies operated in to the types of march that an army can make, the administration and supply for the army and even his thoughts on winter campaigns. In the same year that he wrote his *General Principia vom Kriege* he also wrote two new instructions for the cavalry and the infantry, the *Instruction für die Major Generals von der Cavallerie* and the *Instructions für die Major Generals von der Infanterie*. These instructions were issued to Lieutenant-Generals, who received a copy of both and to Major-Generals who received a copy specific to their arm of service.

The experience of the Austrian army of Maria Theresa was very different. After the War of the Spanish Succession, whilst the Prussian army was drilling and parading before it's King, the Austrian army had been fighting a series of bitter campaigns along its turbulent southern border against the Ottoman Empire. Under the famous Prince Eugene of Savoy, the Austrians at the Battle of Peterwardein (5 August 1716) had defeated and routed the Ottomans, who suffered as many as 30,000 casualties. In 1717 Eugene launched an attack in the fog to defeat the Turks at the Battle of Belgrade (16 August). These victories were to be the zenith of Austrian arms and the successes were not repeated in a later war with the Ottoman Empire from 1736 to 1739. They had failed to build upon their earlier successes and proved to be as inept as their Ottoman foes. By the time peace came in 1739, the Austrians had been driven back into Belgrade and the Ottoman Empire had recovered all the territory it had ceded to Austria in 1718. The initial successes against the Ottoman Empire had dried up and now on the eve of the first of the Silesian Wars, defeat was accepted as the norm and morale low. Although the defeats in the war of 1736–39 could not be overlooked, the raw material, the regimental

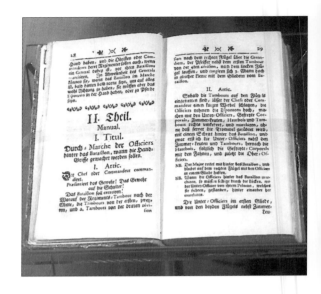

ABOVE **The *Reglement vor die koniglich preussiche Infanterie* was the central authority for any kind of military duties including the drill manuals. The original copy of 1750 belonged to IR41 and includes some additions based on the Silesian Wars experience of the regiment. (PM)**

FAR LEFT **The Prussian army was intensely Lutheran and all regiments had a Field Preacher (*Feldprediger*) to guide them spiritually. They were on the whole young active men who went into battle with their regiments. Frederick stipulated that preachers on being ordained should be 'of good repute, learned, and if possible still wearing their own hair'. The uniform illustrated was prescribed by Frederick in 1742 and closely akin to that of the French *abbé*. (PM)**

LEFT **Fusilier of a 'German' infantry regiment, either Wied-Runckel, Alt-Wolfenbüttel, Browne or Sincere as these four were the only 'German' regiments with scalloped hat lace. This is the standard uniform for 'German' regiments. (Print after Ottenfeld/PH)**

soldier of Maria Theresa's army, was as good as any other. This was demonstrated in the bitter struggles with Prussia during the two Silesian Wars. Nevertheless, as a result of these campaigns a military commission was set up in 1748 under the presidency of Prince Charles of Lorraine to investigate and implement the necessary reforms as a matter of urgency. Two influential members of the commission were Leopold Graf von Daun, who was responsible for the reforms for the infantry, and Joseph Wenzel Prince von Lichtenstein, who concentrated on the artillery. The commission increased troop strength, ensured better training and discipline and a military academy was founded at Wiener Neustadt. With the founding of this academy a new breed of professional officer joined the army. Knowledge and competence were considered to be of greater value than lineage. It was this new, more confident army that took the field against the Prussians in 1756. As the Prussians themselves observed after Lobositz 'these are no longer the same old Austrians'.

ABOVE **Grenadier, fusilier and drummer (sitting on drum) of 'German' regiments. (Print after Ottenfeld/PH)**

BELOW **An illustration of the development of the musket used by Austrian infantry during the 18th century. The *Commiss-Flinte* of 1754 (bottom) was in use at Kolin. (PH)**

The Saxon Army

The middle years of the eighteenth century were not kind to the Saxon army. During the Silesian Wars they had fought bravely but without success. At Hohenfriedeberg they were soundly defeated by the Prussians and at Soor seven more of the army's battalions were on the losing side with the Austrians. The final humiliation came at Kesseldorf (15 December 1745) when the Prussian army under Leopold of Anhalt-Dessau, the 'Old Dessauer', defeated the entire Saxon army of 25,000 men and Austrian allies numbering 7,000 in only a couple of hours' fighting. The Saxon army however did not undergo any major reforms in the inter-war years as Saxony hoped to remain neutral in any future conflict. This was a naïve approach

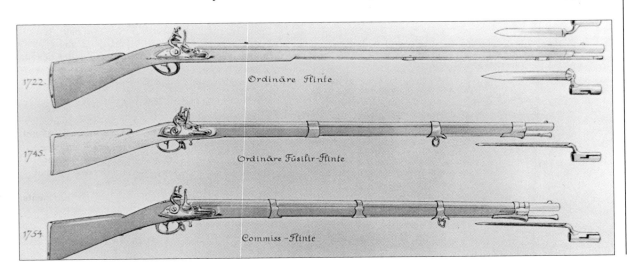

to the defence of their own sovereignty and to dealing with Frederick in particular and culminated in disaster when the bulk of the Saxon army surrendered to the Prussians at Pirna in 1756. Frederick incorporated the majority of the Saxons into the Prussian army, but they were found to be unwilling to serve their Prussian masters and deserted continuously. By the end of 1757 there were only three Saxon infantry regiments and one grenadier battalion still with the Prussian army. The old Saxon army however did not totally disintegrate – the disgruntled soldiers made their way west and re-formed under the command of Prinz Xavier joining their French allies. These Saxon battalions played a significant part in the war against Prussia's allies in the west, Britain, Hanover, Hesse Kassel and Brunswick. They fought bravely and proved to be more than reliable provided they were kept firmly under control by their officers. Among some of the regiments that managed to get away from the camp at Pirna and join the Austrians were four cavalry units, a single cuirassier regiment, the Garde Carabinier and three light cavalry regiments – Prinz Albrecht, Prinz Karl and Graf Brühl. They fought bravely at Kolin and contributed in no small measure to the successes of the Austrian cavalry in the battle.

The elements of the armies

No matter what the nationality the composition of European armies in the eighteenth century was basically similar. They consisted of three elements – infantry, cavalry and artillery. The infantryman made up the bulk of any army, and it was he who had to fight to hold ground to win the battles. The majority of the infantry were musketeer and fusilier regiments. Prussian regiments were normally two battalions in size and approximately 1,700 men strong. In the Austrian army three battalions made up a regiment, with a strength in the region of 2,100 men. Within these formations there were elite organisations most notably the Guard regiments who tended to be the crème de la crème of any army. The Austrian army did not possess Guard regiments, but like other armies they did have grenadier battalions which were normally composite formations made up of the grenadier companies from the musketeer and fusilier regiments and approximately 700 men

ABOVE LEFT **An Austrian Hussar on outpost duty. (Print after Ottenfeld/PH)**

ABOVE RIGHT **Austrian light troops. The mounted figure is from a Grenz (border) Hussar regiment and the foot figure is a private of the Szluiner Croats, who were in the village of Chotzemitz. (Print after Ottenfeld/PH)**

OPPOSITE TOP **Foot officer (left), mounted officer (centre) and grenadier (right) of 'German' infantry. (Print after Ottenfeld/PH)**

OPPOSITE MIDDLE **Austrian cuirassiers of Regt. Stampach and although a picture of a later uniform, 1765, this is very much what Austrian cuirassiers looked like at Kolin where the facing colours were red except for Alt- Modena who had blue. (Print after Ottenfeld/PH)**

OPPOSITE BOTTOM **This picture shows the typical uniform for a 'Hungarian' regiment. This regiment, Gyulai, did not fight at Kolin. IR Haller was at Kolin and had light blue facings and trousers. (Print after Ottenfeld/PH)**

strong. The use of light infantry, such as Jägers and Pandours (Croats), was a new development in the mid-eighteenth century. The Jägers were normally foresters and hunters, recruited for their ability to shoot accurately and act independently. The most feared were the Austrian Croats, who were from the wild eastern borders of the empire. An infantryman's existence was gruelling for no matter the quality and reputation of a regiment, marching on foot was the only means of movement. Battles were fought on average less than once a month and so the majority of the time was spent marching, bivouacking, foraging and if time allowed the infantryman was drilled through the evolutions he was required to master in order to fight effectively in battle. The rigours of campaigning were felt most by the infantryman, rations were normally scarce whilst in camp and more scarce when on the march; the weather and disease took its toll as much as any battle. The long hot and dusty summers of the Seven Years War caused thirst and exhaustion. Armies often wintered in a hostile area, and disease was a constant enemy. Veterans were able to build up their immunity, but with poor medical services the younger, less robust recruit was very likely to succumb to respiratory and digestive diseases. The infantryman in this period certainly was, if he survived, 'as tough as old boots'.

The next largest element and more glamorous arm was the cavalry. Riding into battle they considered themselves the inheritors of the traditions of the medieval knight. In battle they tended to be positioned on the wings of the army. There were three categories of cavalry – heavy (kuirassier and horse), medium (dragoons) and light (hussars, light dragoons and chevauxleger). Regiments were normally divided into four squadrons, but often as many as ten and it was not uncommon for only one or two squadrons of a regiment to be present at a battle. There were on average about 80 troopers per squadron. The heavy cavalry were the shock troops of the army. Riding big horses and with the ability to deliver a devastating charge, they would be committed to battle to exploit a weakness in the enemy line. The dragoons were originally trained to be mounted infantrymen, but over the years this role had declined and more and more often they found themselves being utilised like heavy cavalry. The most famous of the light cavalry were the hussars. They wore extravagant uniforms and generally were led by flamboyant and daring commanders. The light cavalry were trained in reconnaissance duties and to operate behind enemy lines causing as much chaos as possible to the rear areas. In battle they were more often than not pitted against the enemy's light cavalry, competing to harry the flanks of the battle line and if necessary mount a pursuit.

The artillery were the third largest element of any army and the least glamorous, but of vital importance. The administrative unit was the regiment, but in battle artillery operated in companies or batteries consisting of six to ten pieces of ordnance. The officers tended to be technically minded and the men educationally a cut above the other rank and file of the army. The size of a cannon was designated by the weight of shot it fired. The most common field piece was the 6-pdr, but guns as big as the 24-pdr could be used. More often these big guns were employed in sieges. Cannons were heavy pieces that could not be moved quickly when on the march and once positioned for battle not easily redeployed. The job of an artilleryman apart from loading, priming and firing the cannon, required patience and hard physical work. Deployed artillery was vulnerable to counter battery fire, enemy light troops and cavalry. Added to this there was the constant danger of powder explosions caused by sparks or fire.

Armies in the 'Age of Reason' were drawn up in a conventional manner. They had a first line, a second line and a reserve. Within this formation the infantry tended to be placed in the centre with artillery interspersed and cavalry on the flanks. Infantry and cavalry marched to battle in column, but deployed into line to engage the enemy. The line formation allowed an infantry regiment to deliver a greater weight of firepower. Precise procedures varied from army to army, but in general it was the same. The front rank would fire a volley, move to the rear and reload. This allowed the second rank to fire and the procedure would be repeated as many times as there were ranks. It was therefore possible for well-trained troops to deliver 3–5 volleys per minute. The prudent commander did not put all his infantry in the first line, normally a reserve was held 150–300 yards behind this line, ready to advance and reinforce the first line if required, isolate any penetration of the line or provide a rallying point should the line break completely. Cavalry were there to deal with the enemy cavalry. They were ineffective charging a line of steady formed infantry when unsupported. If, however, they were able to catch infantry in the flank they had the potential to destroy them as the infantry would find it difficult to change formation in time to meet the threat. Good cavalry were unable to compensate for the inadequacies of bad infantry and were incapable of winning battles on their own, but an energetic commander would utilise his cavalry to give him more options both defensively and offensively. The role of the artillery was to support the main line of defence or attack and cause as many casualties as possible. To achieve this the artillery fired round shot, literally a round iron ball that would plough through the ranks. There was also the canister round, which was the cannon's equivalent of a shotgun cartridge, each round contained a certain number of small 3oz balls, the 3-pdr

having 50; the 6-pdr 80, the 12-pdr 150 and the 24-pdr 300. The point blank range for these rounds was between 400m for the 3-pdr increasing to 800 metres for the 24-pdr. The artillery were the butchers of the battlefield.

Topography was an important factor in battle as much as the weather and the time of day. A commander had to ensure that the ground selected enabled him to deploy properly; his frontage should not be too extended, causing gaps in his line and thereby weakening it, nor should his battle line be too constricted as this would mean his troops would be unable to deploy in the correct formation. The ground also had to suit each type of arm, with infantry able to occupy most ground, cavalry required fairly open ground and the artillery an unobstructed field of fire allowing them to fire at their effective range. Hills and woods were screens behind which troops could be moved. Features such as steep hills and dense woods were quite often unpassable to troops and as such provided a barrier or a secure flank. Gently undulating terrain provided 'dead' ground which would enable a commander to move troops to reinforce a flank or weak spot or give him the ability to prepare an attack unseen by the enemy. An effective commander could use ground to give his forces an advantage over their enemies.

ABOVE LEFT **Carabinier of the Saxon Garde Carabiniers. This is the campaign uniform, a blackened cuirass was worn under the coat in battle. A red uniform was worn for parades. (MMB)**

ABOVE RIGHT **Austrian artillery. Left is a Buchsenmeister of the 'Netherlands' artillery and right is a fusilier. Note the fusilier is wearing gaiters and not boots, which were normally worn by artillery crews. (Print after Ottenfeld/PH)**

THE SPRING CAMPAIGN AND THE BATTLE OF PRAGUE

The 1756 campaign which had culminated in the victory at Lobositz had not been as successful as Frederick had hoped. Two aims had been achieved – he disposed of the Saxon army and would also be able to use Saxony as a base for any future campaigns. In the field though he had been unable to achieve the decisive victory over the Austrians he had anticipated. In reality Frederick had lost the element of surprise and with it the ability to seize the initiative. The Austrian forces were still intact

PRUSSIAN ADVANCE INTO BOHEMIA, APRIL–MAY 1757

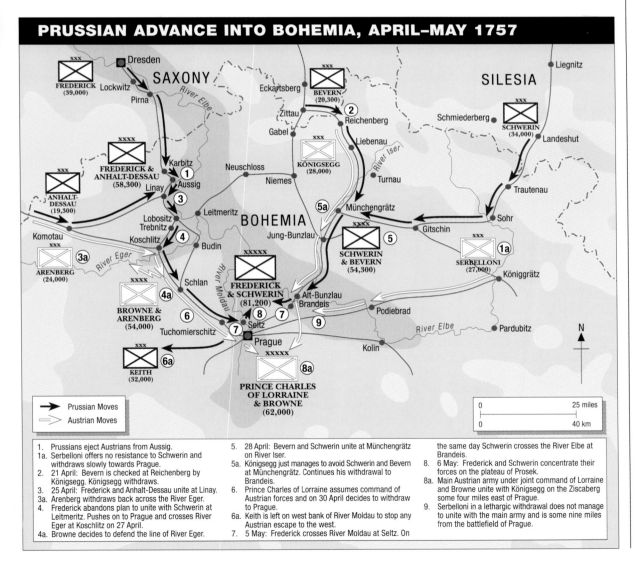

1. Prussians eject Austrians from Aussig.
1a. Serbelloni offers no resistance to Schwerin and withdraws slowly towards Prague.
2. 21 April: Bevern is checked at Reichenberg by Königsegg. Königsegg withdraws.
3. 25 April: Frederick and Anhalt-Dessau unite at Linay.
3a. Arenberg withdraws back across the River Eger.
4. Frederick abandons plan to unite with Schwerin at Leitmeritz. Pushes on to Prague and crosses River Eger at Koschlitz on 27 April.
4a. Browne decides to defend the line of River Eger.

5. 28 April: Bevern and Schwerin unite at Münchengrätz on River Iser.
5a. Königsegg just manages to avoid Schwerin and Bevern at Münchengrätz. Continues his withdrawal to Brandeis.
6. Prince Charles of Lorraine assumes command of Austrian forces and on 30 April decides to withdraw to Prague.
6a. Keith is left on west bank of River Moldau to stop any Austrian escape to the west.
7. 5 May: Frederick crosses River Moldau at Seltz. On

the same day Schwerin crosses the River Elbe at Brandeis.
8. 6 May: Frederick and Schwerin concentrate their forces on the plateau of Prosek.
8a. Main Austrian army under joint command of Lorraine and Browne unite with Königsegg on the Ziscaberg some four miles east of Prague.
9. Serbelloni in a lethargic withdrawal does not manage to unite with the main army and is some nine miles from the battlefield of Prague.

and able to present themselves as the victims, allowing them to conclude their treaties with France and Russia. During the winter months both sides prepared for the forthcoming spring campaign. In January 1757 the Diet of the Empire confirmed its allegiance to the anti-Prussian cause. Maria Theresa was promised 6,000 men by Würzburg, 4,000 by Bavaria, and troops from Cologne (1,800), the Palatinate (6,000) and Württemberg (6,000) marched to aid France. Frederick had only England, Hanover, Hesse-Kassel and Brunswick to assist him in keeping the French and Reichs Army at bay on his western flank. With his allies in the west mobilising to hold the French 'Army of Observation' in check, Frederick felt more secure and was now able to turn his attention to dealing with the Austrians in Bohemia. In early March 1757 Frederick realised that the French were further behind in their preparations than expected and this gave him a vital window of opportunity to fight a war on one front, defeating the Austrians before the French intervened. With a force of 10,000 men co-operating with the Hanoverian forces in the west and 20,000 more in East Prussia, Frederick had 113,000 men at his disposal for the forthcoming campaign.

It seems that Frederick's original policy was to remain on the defensive and wait for the Austrians to attack. This delay would have suited the Austrians, allowing their allies, the Russians and the French, to mobilise and attack Frederick's flanks. In the end Frederick listened to his advisor Hans Karl von Winterfeldt, agreeing that allowing the Austrians to build up their forces in Bohemia where they had important magazines at Königgrätz and Pardubitz represented the greatest threat. His own forces were spread out over a 130-mile front along the Bohemian border from Saxony to Silesia. Frederick decided to attack. His plan was for four columns to strike into Bohemia. In the west Moritz von Anhalt-Dessau (19,300 men) would advance from Chemnitz

An engraving of Frederick the Great at Prague. It shows the Prussian troops, having turned the Austrian right flank, advancing against Marshal Browne between the Homoleberg and the Taborberg. Prague can be seen in the distance. (ASKB)

in Saxony down the River Eger, meanwhile Frederick with the main army (39,600) would advance directly on Prague from Dresden, down the west bank of the River Elbe and join with Anhalt-Dessau at Linnay. The other two columns would see August Wilhelm, Duke of Bevern (20,300) cross into Bohemia from Lusatia and advance via Reichenberg and Münchengrätz down the River Iser and unite with Field Marshal Schwerin (34,000) coming from Silesia marching westwards by way of Trautenau and Sobotka. The final two columns would then concentrate near Leitmeritz, north-west of Prague on the Elbe. Frederick was in luck as the Austrian commander had changed, with Prince Charles of Lorraine replacing the far more able Field Marshal von Browne. Browne had not planned for a defensive campaign and as such had prepared magazines near the frontier. The Austrians were deployed in four separate areas, Serbelloni with 27,000 men was the most easterly, based on Königgrätz to watch Schwerin. Königsegg facing Bevern, had 28,000 troops with him around Reichenberg in northern Bohemia on the border with Lusatia, while Browne was located between Prague and the River Eger with 30,000 men. Finally, Arenberg had 24,000 men near Plan in the west. These dispositions were not ideal for Browne's planned offensive – they were hopelessly inadequate when the cautious and indecisive Prince Charles assumed command.

Prior to the advance Frederick's plans remained a closely guarded secret. The only aggressive actions taken by the Prussians were the raids carried out by Anhalt-Dessau and Bevern in their sectors of the front. This deception plan lulled the Austrians and they were taken completely by surprise when Frederick launched his attack into Bohemia on 18 April 1757. Once again he had managed to achieve surprise – now the Prussians had to achieve a concentration of force and in this Frederick was once again helped by Austrian indecisiveness. Schwerin was the first to move, crossing the Riesengebirge on 18 April. As planned he moved west via Trautenau and Sobotka to link up with Bevern. Serbelloni, deployed to protect the magazines at Königgrätz and Pardubitz, made no effort to impede Schwerin and instead withdrew in a particularly disinterested manner westwards towards Prague. Serbelloni was so slow in his withdrawal that he was still some nine miles away from the battlefield of Prague on the day of the battle. He had covered barely 65 miles in 17 days of marching. Bevern and Schwerin duly joined forces on 28 April at Münchengrätz. At their meeting Bevern was able to bring Schwerin up to date with his advance and the engagement he had had against Königsegg at Reichenberg. Bevern had begun his advance on 20 April and within a day had encountered his first resistance. Königsegg, a far more adventurous commander than Serbelloni, immediately moved to engage Bevern. The small Battle of Reichenberg was fought on 21 April. Although Königsegg chose an excellent position amongst small brooks and forested hills, he soon found his left wing being assaulted by Bevern, and after brief but fierce fighting Bevern succeeded in turning Königsegg out of the position. Königsegg, having been bold enough to confront Bevern, but let down by Serbelloni's refusal to do the same against Schwerin, now found he had to outmarch both Schwerin and Bevern to avoid being trapped between their two forces. Having avoided Schwerin at Münchengrätz, he continued his retreat down the Iser to defend the bridges across the Elbe at Brandeis.

What of Frederick and Anhalt-Dessau? Frederick moved on the 20 April and passed the Mittelgebirge without opposition. By 25 April he was at Linnay, his rendezvous with Anhalt-Dessau. Frederick's plan was going well, for on the same day Anhalt-Dessau marched into his camp, having had the occasional brush with Arenburg's Austrian forces. Indeed Arenburg was still on the line of the Eger encamped at Budin, with the intention of delaying any Prussian advance. Frederick now changed his plan and instead of concentrating his forces at Leitmeritz with Schwerin/Bevern, as planned, he decided to press on to Prague. The Austrians under Field Marshal Browne, for Prince Charles had not arrived, were determined to make a stand on the line of the Eger. The Prussians, however, marching through the night of 26 April, turned their left flank and crossed the Eger using pontoons at Koschtitz, in the early hours of the morning of 27 April. The Prussians climbed the tree-covered Budin ridge, and expecting the Austrians to make a stand were surprised to meet no opposition. On reaching the crest they could see the dust clouds of the withdrawing Austrians heading south-east. The Prussians descended the ridge and followed on behind the withdrawing Austrians. On 28 April Frederick had his headquarters in the village of Charwatetz and on the same day learned of the successful union of Schwerin and Bevern. The Austrians had abandoned Budin with little effort to remove or destroy it's ample supplies and Frederick, delighted at this windfall, now had enough to go all the way to Prague. The columns had united as planned and now sought to bring the Austrians to battle. Prince Charles of Lorraine finally arrived to take command of the Austrian forces on 29 April. There was little love lost between Browne and Prince Charles and they almost came to blows deciding what the Austrian strategy should be. Browne favoured confronting Frederick and with almost equal forces – 58,000 Austrians and a good position against

Prince Henry wades into the Rocketnitzer-Bach to give encouragement to Infantry Regiment No. 13 (Itzenplitz). Prince Henry did this time and again at Prague and, not surprisingly, spent most of the battle wet through. (Print after Carl Rochling)

54,000 Prussians – was convinced that they could defeat the Prussian king. Prince Charles, a cautious and unimaginative commander, disagreed and wanted to withdraw to safety around Prague. Prince Charles had his way and on 30 April orders were issued for the withdrawal. Frederick, keeping the pressure on the Austrians, followed up and on the 1 May was within a day's march of Prague. Meanwhile the Schwerin/Bevern column followed Königsegg along the road to Brandeis. Their crossing of the river was delayed however as Königsegg had destroyed the bridges across the Elbe. Frederick reached Prague with his advance guard on 2 May, closely followed by the main body on 3 May, a day of sunshine and showers. With Croats manning the ramparts, those Prussian officers who looked beyond the walls of Prague would have seen the white-coated lines of the Austrians on the Ziscaberg to the east. With Schwerin unable to cross the Elbe until 5 May, a bold commander would have taken the opportunity to attack Frederick whilst he was outnumbered and his nearest reinforcements still beyond the Elbe. Once again Frederick profited from Austrian timidity. He was able to reconnoitre the Moldau, find a suitable crossing point at Seltz, span the river with a pontoon bridge and cross unopposed on 5 May. At the same time he sent word to Schwerin that he should cross the Elbe with all speed and join with the main army on the plateau of Prosek some three miles north of the Austrian position. Frederick, having left Marshal Keith with 32,000 men on the west bank of the Moldau to stop any Austrian escape, decided to attack the Austrians with all speed and this was planned for 6 May.

The death of Marshal Schwerin at the Battle of Prague. Schwerin saw his own regiment (No.24) falter and seizing the colour exclaimed, 'Come on, children, come on!' he went a few yards further and was promptly hit by canister shot and fell dead. (Print after Richard Knotel)

THE BATTLE OF PRAGUE

Frederick gave orders for the Prussians to strike camp and be on the march by 5.00am. By 6.30am Schwerin had united with Frederick and formed the left wing of the Prussian army. Reunited with his trusted Lieutenant, Frederick spent some time observing the Austrian lines from the highest point on the Prosek ridge. The Austrian position had its left wing, commanded by Prince Charles, anchored to the Ziscaberg and stretched eastwards along the plateau above the Rocketnitzer Bach with their right wing, commanded by Browne, on the forward slopes of the Taborberg. After consideration Frederick ruled out a frontal attack, for with the Austrian position protected by the Rocketnitzer Bach and valley, which was enough of an obstacle to disorganise any attack, even the well-drilled Prussians would find the task difficult. After a reconnaissance it was discovered that in the east the plateau sloped down to some green meadows which looked better ground for an attack. Frederick resolved to turn the Austrian right flank and gave orders for the march eastwards, but to attack the Austrian right the Prussians had to swing south and attack through the villages of Kej, Hostawitz and Unter Poczernitz, cross the Rocketnitzer Bach and then advance westwards with Sterbohol on their left, up the slope between the Taborberg and the Homoleberg, towards Maleschitz.

At about 10.00am the Austrians realised what the Prussians intended to do and Browne, who had gathered all the grenadier companies from his line regiments into a reserve of 40 companies, moved them speedily to the right flank. A large mass of cavalry, 12 regiments of cuirassiers and dragoons and five weak regiments of hussars, were deployed to cover the new right flank at a gap between Sterbohol and a large pond to the south of the village. Schwerin, who was leading the Prussians around to their attack positions, determined to strike 'while the iron was hot' and as a result Prussian troops were thrown into the assault as they arrived. The first to arrive were 20 squadrons of Schönaich's command and without delay they were fed into a cavalry battle with the Austrian's near Sterbohol. This battle was long and indecisive, raging backwards and forwards. The Austrian grenadiers arrived and took up their position to the north of Sterbohol, meanwhile the leading Prussian artillery had become stuck fast in Ünter-Poczernitz. This forced the first line of Prussian infantry on the left wing out wide of the village and on to what they had thought were meadows. They were soon up to their knees and in some cases waists, in soft black silt. They were not meadows after all, but the drained beds of fishponds whose greenness came from shoots of oats, which fish would feed on when the ponds were refilled with water and restocked with carp. Browne had been moving more infantry and artillery to his west and there must have been some amused faces, at the Prussian infantryman's discomfort, amongst the Austrians as they arrived to form a new line on the eastern slopes of the plateau. The business was however going to get far more serious.

Schwerin was urging his men on into the attack and although Frederick arrived on the scene and questioned the wisdom of launching piecemeal unsupported attacks, the 14 battalions of the first line of the left wing continued their march. Austrian artillery on the Homoleberg opened fire on the advancing Prussians and did terrible carnage. Frederick witnessed the infantry regiments (IR) 37 (Kurssell) and

An engraving of the siege of Prague. The city was not well provisioned and had Frederick persevered with the siege and trusted Bevern to keep Daun at bay, Prague would have capitulated with serious consequences for Maria Theresa. (ASKB)

33 (Fouqué) flee in disorder. The attack was an unmitigated disaster, with the Austrians firing controlled volleys and the artillery raking the Prussians with canister, the remaining eight battalions of the first line gave way. Further disaster was about to strike the Prussians for at about 11.00am General Winterfeldt was riding at the head of IR24 (Schwerin) when he was struck in the neck by a ball and fell from his horse wounded. Schwerin seeing this rode up and had Winterfeldt lifted on to a spare horse. Sensing panic in the men of IR24, his own regiment, he grabbed a green regimental colour of the second battalion and rode to the front of the regiment exhorting them to follow him. He had ridden no more than a few yards when he was shattered by canister and fell to the ground dead. The Austrians counter-attacked down the slope to push back the 14 battalions of the dead Schwerin's second line, but as they did so a gap opened up on their left flank, in the angle between the redeployed right wing and the main force, which still faced north. Lieutenant-General Hautcharmoy led a force of some 22 battalions into this gap. He led six battalions of the Infantry Regiments 26 (Meyernick), 28 (Hautcharmoy) and 32 (Tresckow) with the Duke of Bevern in nominal command of the remaining battalions. Many regimental commanders found their own way through the ponds and spurs to carry out their orders and a small group of battalions found themselves advancing through two ponds near Kej and up on to the plateau amid an eerie silence on the battlefield. To their relief they found the exposed left wing of the Austrian infantry who were giving Schwerin's old command a hard time. A battalion of IR12 (Darmstädt) wheeled to their left, followed by two battalions each of regiments 18 (Prince von Preüssen) and 30 (Kannacher). This small force began to roll up the Austrian's from the left in quick succession. The first to feel the effect of this new attack was the Austrian Infantry Regiment Wied, followed by a Mainz Kreis regiment. While this infantry battle had been going on, the cavalry battle to the south of Sterbohol had been raging back and forth and at about 11.30am Lieutenant-General Zieten appeared with 20 fresh

squadrons of hussars and five of dragoons. He led them to the south of the ponds, joining the 4th (Puttkamer) and 6th (Werner) Hussars and launched an attack into the exposed right wing of the Austrian cavalry. The Austrian cavalry wavered and finally crumbled.

With the Prussian infantry rolling up their left flank and the cavalry effectively scattered over Bohemia, the Austrian right wing was in perilous danger. The final blow was when Browne, the one man who might have rescued the situation, was struck by a cannon shot and thrown to the ground mortally wounded. The wing collapsed, and being cut off from the main position they escaped in the direction of Beneschau. It was midday and the Prussian breakthrough in the north was about to assault the exposed right wing of the main Austrian position. The remaining 14 battalions of Hautcharmoy and Bevern continued with their advance up the slope into the gap and against the Austrian right. At the same time the Austrians in the earthworks between the ponds at Kej and Hlaupetin were dislodged by Major-General Manstein leading four battalions of grenadiers. Slowly but surely the Austrians found themselves being pushed back on the northern edge of the plateau. General Kheul rallied the Austrians and formed a new line on the eastern side of a steep little valley, running north from Malleschitz across the Kaiser Strasse to the village of Hrdlorzez on a bend in the Rocketnitzer Bach. The fighting now became desperate and was some of the heaviest of the day, as the Austrians were determined not to be dislodged from this new position. The Prussian IR1 (Winterfeldt) was destroyed as it tried to climb the steep slope from the bottom of the valley. The Prussians on the far right of their main line were not idle either. Prince Henry led IR13 (Itzenplitz) across the Rocketnitzer Bach, only to almost disappear as his diminutive form sank into the water almost from sight. The Regiment however followed his example and soon a soaking wet Prince Henry was urging on his battalions, as they attacked the Austrian left flank. Once again it was only because their flanks were being turned that the Austrians gave ground to the Prussians; Prince Henry in the east, Manstein in the west and Frederick with Zieten from the south-east. At 3.00pm the Austrians withdrew on Prague and safety. The Austrian cavalry had earned for themselves an excellent reputation in their previous battles against Frederick and once again they showed themselves to be brave and determined men, as they launched attack and counter-attack against the advancing Prussians. But for the Austrians it was too late, the day was lost. The majority of the Austrians ended up in Prague with in the region of 3,000 scattering into the Bohemian countryside. Once again the Prussians were forced to recognise that the Austrians had acquitted themselves well and showed that their performance at Lobositz the previous year was no flash in the pan. The Battle of Prague had been a costly victory for Frederick, the Prussians suffered nearly 14,000 casualties while the Austrians had lost 8,800 men and a further 4,500 as prisoners. For Frederick, however, as he rode across the battlefield the next day, the true realisation of the cost of his victory came home. He had lost Major-Generals Schöning and Blankensee, Lieutenant-General Hautcharmoy and most saddening of all his great friend and ally Field Marshal Schwerin. Most disturbingly Frederick had also lost many veterans from his infantry and for the first time some of his battalions had fled in battle.

ORDERS OF BATTLE, THE BATTLE OF KOLIN, 18TH JUNE 1757

Uniforms of the Saxon regiments at Kolin.
L–R: Trooper Saxon Garde Carabinier, Corporal Chevauxleger Regiment Prinz Albrecht, Drummer Chevauxleger Regiment Prinz Karl and a Colonel of the Graf Brühl Chevauxleger Regiment. All four regiments took a major part in the battle and fought with great distinction. (Wolfgang Friedrich/ Author's collection)

Army organisation in the Seven Years War

During the Seven Years War armies rarely, if ever, had a formalised command structure. There were no fixed brigades, divisions, or corps. Rather on the day of battle the commander-in-chief would allocate troops to each commander depending on his task for the coming battle. Armies were frequently divided into 'wings' and a senior commander would be appointed to take control of a wing and direct its operations. A 'wing' could simply refer to a formation of a number of men and so an army might easily consist of a number of 'wings', depending on the commander's plan. A corps of men was almost literal in its translation in that it was a 'body' of men.

THE AUSTRIAN ARMY

Commander in Chief:
Field Marshal (FM) Leopold Graf von Daun

Light Troops

General of Cavalry (GdK) Franz Graf Nadasty, Ban von Croatia

Lieutenant General (FmL) Freiherr von Morocz
Festetic Hussars – 6 sqns
Morocz Hussars – 6 sqns
Kommandierten Line Cavalry – 1,000 men (KOM)
Dessewffly Hussars – 1 sqn
Kaiser Hussars – 3 sqns

Saxons:
Prinz Albert Chevauxleger – 4 sqns (PRA)
Prinz Karl Chevauxleger – 4 sqns (PRK)
Graf Brühl Chevauxleger – 4 sqns (GRB)

Major General (GFwM) Freiherr von Beck
Karlstadter Hussars – 2 sqns
Banalisten Hussars – 2 sqns
Kaiser Hussars – 3 sqns
Warasdiner Hussars – 1 sqn
Warasdiner-Kreutz Grenzer – 1 bn
Gradiskaner Grenzer – 2 bns
Broder Grenzer – 2 bns
Kommodantierten Line – 1 bn

FmL Graf von Hadik
Nadasty Hussars – 5 sqns
Hadik Hussars – 2 sqns
Kalnoky Hussars – 6 sqns
Jazygier Hussars – 5 sqns
Baranyay Hussars – 1 sqns
Splenyi Hussars – 2 sqns
Esterhazy Hussars – 2 sqns

Cavalry Wings

GdK Johann Baptist Graf Serbelloni

FmL Benedict Graf von Daun
Kalkreuth Cuirassiers – 6 sqns (KAL)
Kolowrat Dragoons – 6 sqns (KOL)
Savoyen Dragoons – 6 sqns (SAV)

FmL Graf O'Donnell
De Ligne Dragoons – 6 sqns (LIG)
Schmerzing Cuirassiers – 6 sqns (SCH)
Portugal Cuirassiers – 6 sqns (PRT)

GdK Graf Stampach

FmL Graf Kolowrat
Serbelloni Cuirassiers – 6 sqns (SER)
Porporati Dragoons – 5 sqns (PORP)
Hesse-Darmstadt Dragoons – 4 sqns (H-D)

FmL Freiherr von Wollwarth
Gelhay Cuirassiers – 6 sqns (GEL)
Alt-Modena Cuirassiers – 6 sqns (A-M)
Saxe-Gotha Dragoons – 6 sqns (S-G)

Infantry Wings

General of Infantry (FzM) Ernst Dietrich Freiherr von Marschall

FmL Andlau
Erzherzog Karl Infantry Regiment – 2 bns (EKR)
Moltke Infantry Regiment – 3 bns (MOL)
Puebla Infantry Regiment – 3 bns (PUE)

FmL Graf von Starhemberg
Haller Infantry Regiment – 2 bns (HAL)
Gaisruck Infantry Regiment – 2 bns (GAI)
Neipperg Infantry Regiment – 3 bns (NEI)

FzM Graf von Colloredo

FmL von Puebla
Arhemberg Infantry Regiment – 3 bns (ARH)
Thurheim Infantry Regiment – 3 bns (THU)
Leopold Daun Infantry Regiment – 3 bns (LDA)
Harsch Infantry Regiment – 2 bns (HAR)

FmL Freiherr von Sincere
Deuchmeister Infantry Regiment – 2 bns (DEU)
Baden-Baden Infantry Regiment – 2 bns (B-B)
Botta Infantry Regiment – 3 bns (BOT)

Independent Commands

FmL Graf zu Wied
Los Rios Infantry Regiment – 1 bn (L-R)
Salm-Salm Infantry Regiment – 2 bns (SAL)
Platz Infantry Regiment – 1 bn (PLA)
Starhemberg Infantry Regiment – 1 bn (STA)
d'Arberg Infantry Regiment – 1 bn (ARB)
Saxe-Gotha Infantry Regiment – 1 bn (S-G)
Mercy Infantry Regiment – 1 bn (MER)
Prince de Ligne Infantry Regiment – 1 bn (LIG)
Wurttemberg Cuirassiers – 6 sqns (WUR)
Birkenfeld Cuirassiers – 6 sqns (BIR)

GFzM Marquis Castiglione
Jung-Modena Dragoons – 4 sqns (J-M)
O'Donnell Cuirassiers – 6 sqns (ODO)
Saxon Garde Carabiniers – 2 sqns (SGC)

Independent Units
Infantry:
Fiorenza Grenadier Battalion – 1 bn (FIOR)
Soro Grenadier Battalion – 1 bn (SOR)
Banalisten Grenzers – 2 bns
Szluiner Grenzer – 2 bns
Cavalry:
Burghausen Elite Regiment
Panovsky Elite Regiment
Artillery:
2 x howitzer batteries (bty)
2 x 12-pdr btys,
5 x 6-pdr btys
6 x 3-pdr btys.

THE PRUSSIAN ARMY

Commander in Chief:
King Frederick II of Prussia

Nominated Second-in-Command:
General of Infantry (GdI) Moritz Fürst von Anhalt-Dessau

Advance Guard
Lieutenant-General (GLt) Hans Joachim von Zieten

Major-General (GM) Karl von Katte
Zieten Hussars – 10 sqns
Werner Hussars – 10 sqns
Puttkamer Hussars – 10 sqns
Szekely Hussars – 5 sqns
Seydlitz Hussars – 5 sqns
Wartenberg Hussars – 10 sqns

GM Johann Dietrich von Hülsen
Regiment No. 29 Schultze – 2 bns (29)
Regiment No. 36 Münchow – 2 bns (36)
11th Dragoons Stechow – 5 sqns (D11)

Cavalry Wing
GLt Peter Ernst von Pennavaire

GM Christian Siegfried von Krosigk
8th Cuirassiers Rochow – 5 sqns (C8),
1st Dragoons Normann – 5 sqns (D1),
2nd Cuirassiers Prinz von Preussen – 5 sqns (C2)

GM Anton Friedrich von Krockow
11th Cuirassiers LeibKarabinier – 5 sqns (C11)
3rd Leib Cuirassiers – 5 sqns (C3)

GM George Philipp von Schönaich
13th Cuirassiers Garde du Corps – 3 sqns (C13)
7th Cuirassiers Driesen – 5 sqns (C7)
3rd Dragoons Meinicke – 5 sqns (D3)
6th Cuirassiers Schönaich – 5 sqns (C6)

GM Karl Ludwig von Normann
4th Dragoons Katte – 5 sqns (D4)
2nd Dragoons Blanckensee – 5 sqns (D2)

GM Peter von Meinicke
12th Cuirassiers Kyau – 5 sqns (C12),
1st Cuirassiers Krockow – 5 sqns (C1)

Infantry Wings
GLt Joachim Friedrich von Tresckow

GM Friedrich Franz Herzog von Braunschweig–Luneberg (Wolfenbüttel)
Regiment No. 21 Hülsen – 2 bns (21),
Regiment No. 7 Alt-Bevern – 2 bns (7)

GM Karl Ludwig von Ingersleben
Regiment No. 41 Wied – 2 bns (41),
Regiment No. 35 Prinz Heinrich – 2 bns (35)

GLt August Wilhelm Herzog von Braunschweig-Luneberg (Bevern)

GM Gottlieb Ernst von Pannwitz
Regiment No. 3 Anhalt – 2 bns (3)
Regiment No. 20 Bornstedt – 2 bns (20)

GM Christoph Hermann von Manstein
Regiment No. 17 Manteuffel – 2 bns (17)
Regiment No. 25 Kalkstein – 2 bns (25)
Regiment No. 22 Fürst Moritz – 2 bns (22)

GM Martin Anton Freiherr von Puttkamer
1st Battalion, Regiment No. 15 Leibgarde – 1 bn (15)
Regiment No. 40 Kreytzen – 2 bns (40)
Gemmingen Grenadier Battalion (grenadier companies
from IRs 41/44) – 1 bn (41/44)

Independent units
Infantry:
Fink Grenadier Bn – 1 bn (13/26),
Woldow Gren Bn – 1 bn (12/39),
Nymschöfsky Gren Bn – 1 bn (33/42),
Möllendorf Gren Bn – 1 bn (9/10),
Kahlden Gren Bn (Standing Gren Bn No.1) –
1 bn (Stg 1), Wangenheim Gren Bn – 1 bn (47/gb7)
Artillery:
1 x mortar battery (bty)
1 x howitzer bty
5 x 12-pdr btys
3 x 6-pdr batteries.

Notes:

1. The approximate size of each force on the field was:
   Prussian: Infantry: 19,500; Cavalry: 14,000;
   Artillery: 90 cannon/500 personnel
   Total: 34,000 men
   Austrian: Infantry: 34,000; Cavalry: 17,700;
   Artillery: 154 cannon/1,050 personnel
   Total 52,750 men

2. Precise returns for the various regiments in each army
   do not exist. We can, however, estimate the size of a
   battalion of infantry or regiment of cavalry. On the day of
   the battle the Prussians fielded 32 battalions of infantry
   for a total of 19,500 men and 20 regiments of cavalry at
   14,000 men – approximately 609 men per infantry
   battalion and 700 per cavalry regiment. The Austrians
   fielded 54 battalions of infantry for a total of 34,000 men
   and 38 cavalry regiments at 17,700 – 629 men per
   infantry battalion, 465 men per cavalry regiment.

3. The abbreviation in parentheses is used to identify the
   unit on the map on p.51 *The Initial Prussian Attack*. eg.
   Deuchmeister Infantry Regiment = DEU

4. The losses for each side were as follows:
   Austria: 359 officers, 9,000 men (all casualties),
   5 regimental colours and one cavalry standard.
   Prussia: 281 officers, 9,428 men, 22 regimental colours
   and 45 cannon. The Prussians also lost 115 officers and
   3,968 men, mostly wounded, as prisoners of war.

THE BATTLE OF KOLIN

After the Battle of Prague, Frederick was delighted to discover that the majority of the defeated Austrians had not escaped into the Bohemian countryside, but were trapped inside Prague. He estimated that it would not be long before the provisions in Prague ran out and to speed the process he ordered up the siege train from Leitmeritz. While Frederick waited for his siege train to arrive down the Elbe, news of the defeat at Prague had reached the court in Vienna. Field Marshal Daun, who had been entrusted with the command of Austrian troops in eastern Bohemia, only two days before the battle on 4 May, was now ordered to gather any fugitives from the battle and relieve Prague. Chancellor Kaunitz in Vienna immediately sent a communication to Prince Charles in Prague. Kaunitz told the beleaguered Prince to remain in Prague and wait for Daun to come to his aid. The indecisive Prince was now in sole command, for Browne was dying from the wound he had received in the battle.

Meanwhile Frederick, only too aware of the Austrian plan to relieve Prague, ordered Bevern to hold the Austrians under Daun at bay. Bevern departed the Prussian camp on 10 May with 18,000 men, one of his first tasks being to clear the Croats, who were raiding up the Elbe, from

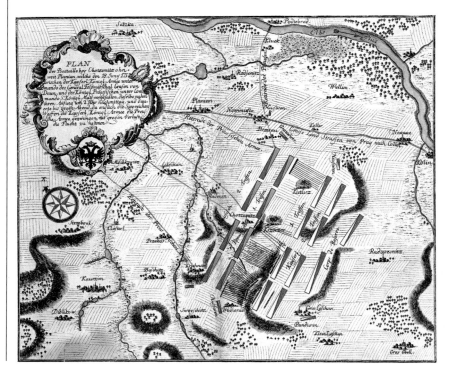

This contemporary map shows the 'accurate' positions and actions of the battle of Chotzemitz (Kolin). Interestingly the famous oak wood is not marked. Like so many maps drawn by those who were not at the battle it is not accurate. (MSW)

THE APPROACH MARCHES TO KOLIN, 12–17 JUNE 1757

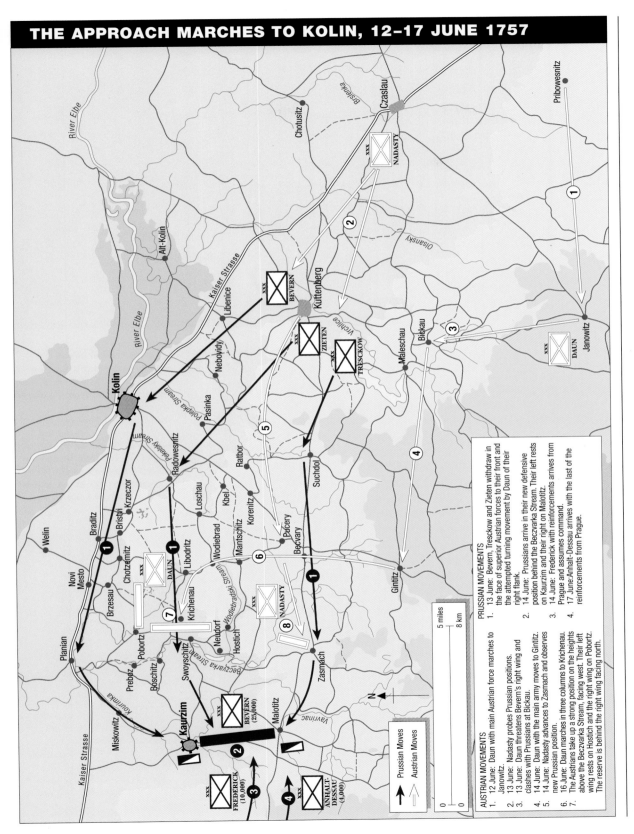

AUSTRIAN MOVEMENTS

1. 12 June: Daun with main Austrian force marches to Janowitz.
2. 13 June: Nadasty probes Prussian positions.
3. 13 June: Daun threatens Bevern's right wing and clashes with Prussians at Bickau.
4. 14 June: Daun with the main army moves to Gintitz.
5. 14 June: Nadasty advances to Zasmach and observes new Prussian position.
6. 16 June: Daun marches in three columns to Krichenau.
7. The Austrians take up a strong position on the heights above the Beczvarka Stream, facing west. Their left wing rests on Hostich and the right wing on Poborz. The reserve is behind the right wing facing north.

PRUSSIAN MOVEMENTS

1. 13 June: Bevern, Tresckow and Zieten withdraw in the face of superior Austrian forces to their front and the attempted turning movement by Daun of their right flank.
2. 13 June: Prussians arrive in their new defensive position behind the Beczvarka Stream. Their left rests on Kaurzim and their right on Malotitz.
3. 14 June: Frederick with reinforcements arrives from Prague and assumes command.
4. 17 June:Anhalt-Dessau arrives with the last of the reinforcements from Prague.

Prussian Moves

Austrian Moves

5 miles

8 km

43

Brandeis and then push any Austrian forces back down the Kaiser Strasse. At Prague, a rocket fired into the air on 29 May signalled the beginning of the bombardment and 60 cannon and mortars opened fire. By 4 June however Frederick began to realise that the bombardment was having little effect. He presumed that Prague was much better stocked than he had at first thought. What Frederick did not know was that Prince Charles had managed to get a message to Daun telling him that there were only enough provisions inside the city to last until 20 June and not until the end of July as Frederick thought. Daun now needed to execute urgently the order he had received from Vienna on 7 June to give battle and relieve Prague. The bombardment continued, but Frederick was more concerned with the manoeuvres of Bevern and Daun. Bevern had been reinforced to 24,000 men. Facing him, however, Daun had managed to put together an army of nearly 60,000. On 9 June the bombardment of Prague effectively ended, the shelling subsequently being desultory. Frederick as a precaution decided to join Bevern and on 13 June he marched with a reinforcement of four battalions of infantry, 16 squadrons of cavalry and 15 cannon. Frederick was not seeking battle when he set out, but was determined to keep Daun in eastern Bohemia.

Frederick had been told by Austrian deserters that Daun was a cautious man who was unlikely to risk a battle to save the city. Frederick's surprise was therefore that much greater when on the night of 13 June he received a message from Bevern informing him that Daun had begun to advance on 12 June with the whole of the Austrian corps under his command. Daun was indeed on the move. Bevern's Corps was six miles south east of Kolin, with its centre on Küttenberg. His right was at Maleschau, with picquets in Bickau. The nearest Austrians were at Czaslau, six miles away to the south-east, under the command of General Graf Nadasty. The main Austrian army was with Daun at Jenkinau and on 12 June he moved his force to Janowitz. Daun's plan was to turn Bevern's right flank while Nadasty held the Prussian commanders attention by probing and demonstrating against his front. On 13 June Daun began his advance from Janowitz and it was not long before the leading Austrian light troops clashed with the Prussian picquets in Bickau. Bevern however was not going to risk the wrath of Frederick by being outflanked by Daun and possibly destroyed. He gave orders for the Prussians to withdraw to a better position closer to Prague, where Frederick would be able to reinforce him.

An engraving that shows two aspects of the battle in a very stylised form. The picture is from the Austrian viewpoint. Firstly we see clearly the original dispositions of Daun with Wied's division facing west over the Beczvarka Stream on the left of the picture and then we see the attack by Hulsen through Krzeczor, which is in the centre just to the left of Kolin on the right. (MSW)

The Prussians withdrew in three columns: Tresckow, the most southerly, went via Suchdol and Zasmach to Malotitz; Zieten took the central route via Radowesnitz and Krichenau to Kaurzim, while Bevern was the most northerly, following the Kaiser Strasse as far as Planian and then down to Kaurzim. The Prussians marched all night on 13 June and arrived in their new position the next day. Bevern now took up a strong defensive position, behind the Beczvarka Stream with his left resting on the fortified town of Kaurzim and his right on Malotitz.

The first Austrians to see the new Prussian position were those of Nadasty who arrived at Zasmach on the 14 June and began their reconnaissance to examine the strength of the Prussian position. Frederick continued his march on 14 June and having had to avoid some Austrian cavalry near Zdantiz finally made his way to Malotitz, where he linked up with Tresckow and Bevern, who arrived with the rest of his command. Having debriefed Bevern, Frederick wasted no time in sending for Anhalt-Dessau to bring as many troops as could be spared from the siege of Prague.

On 15 June the Prussian army rested in their positions and in the warm summer sunshine Frederick found it difficult to believe that Daun was in the country on the other side of the Beczvarka Stream. This is surprising when one considers he had only just managed to escape capture by some Austrian cavalry the previous day and he had received reports from an officer of his Guides that there were Austrian tents in the area of Zasmach. These reports he dismissed. Daun meanwhile, having marched at a leisurely pace via Gintitz (14 June) arrived in his new headquarters at Krichenau on 16 June. As the Austrian army took up a strong position on the heights above the Beczvarka Stream, their right resting on Pobortz in the north while their left was on Hostich, tension was rising in Malotitz as the Prussians realised that Daun was indeed in the hills beyond the Stream and that it was highly likely another battle was to be fought, barely a month after Prague. On 16 June Anhalt-Dessau arrived in Malotitz with the final reinforcements from Prague. Bevern was advising Frederick against attacking Daun when Anhalt-Dessau arrived at Frederick's headquarters and on being asked his opinion exclaimed that Frederick alone was worth some 50,000 men. It was Daun who had closer to 50,000 men whereas Frederick was about to give battle with at most 35,000.

Frederick on looking across the Beczvarka Stream quickly came to the conclusion that Daun was in an almost impregnable position. The streams and dried-up ponds, he well remembered from Prague, would disorganise his infantry and the ground certainly did not favour his

Frederick observes the Austrian positions before the battle from the inn 'Novi Mesto'. The inn 'Zlate Slunce' did not exist in 1757. The inn of that name now was called the 'U slunce' in 1757 and Frederick did not visit the inn. (Engraving after Menzel/PH)

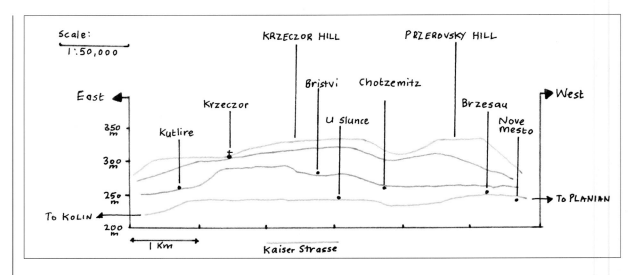

A section looking south, showing the lie of the land, the location of the villages and the Kaiser Strasse with their height above sea level. (Author's collection)

cavalry. Added to this the Prussian position was awkward. His camp was backed up against high ground, the ponds and generally damp conditions to his front did offer some protection, but his right wing was poorly supported and could easily be turned by Daun. This would mean the entire Prussian army being attacked in the flank with possibly disastrous consequences. Frederick also had to consider the need to protect the magazines and Brandeis and Nimburg, which provided his army with its bread. There was also the need to protect the forces besieging Prague. Frederick decided to march north towards Planian and then turn east and march down the Kaiser Strasse, towards Kolin. There he believed he would find open ground and be able to turn Daun's right flank. The ground was not unknown to Frederick as he had fought Chotusitz in 1742 only ten miles south-east of Kolin, however the maps made of the area at this time had been misplaced. Daun on the other hand knew the lie of the land only too well. The Austrians had carried out their annual autumn manoeuvres on this very ground in 1756. During the late afternoon of 17 June Daun watched Frederick's army move northwards in two columns. He watched the Prussians with interest and at 7.00pm ordered his army to break camp and to counter- march to the right. During the night while the Prussians continued their march in two columns northwards towards Planian the Austrian army re-deployed so that at about 5.00am as the sun rose on the morning of 18 June the Austrian deployment took the form of a dog leg with the main position facing north with a frontage of four kilometres and Wied with his division forming the dog leg facing west across the Beczvarka Stream, running south, for $2\frac{1}{2}$ kilometres,

The site of the 'U slunce' in Braditz (modern-day Zlate Slunce) on the day of the battle. (Author)

An inaccurate Panorama of the battle by Augustus Querfurt. We are looking at the battle from behind the Austrian position. The Oak Wood can be identified on the right. (HGM)

from the heights at Pobortz to the village of Swoyschitz. The first line of the main position had the division of Puebla, 11 battalions, on the left on the heights near the village of Pobortz and Andlau with his eight battalions was on the Przerovsky Hill, 1½km eastwards; between the two of them Daun had placed Stampach with six regiments of cavalry and on the far right Serbelloni was forming the new right flank with the six cavalry regiments of his wing. In the second line behind Puebla was Sincere with seven battalions, Castiglione with three cavalry regiments was behind Stampach and forming the second line behind Andlau was Starhemberg with his seven battalions. Daun designated Wied to be his reserve. Daun had also detached Beck to shadow the Prussian movement along the Beczvarka Stream and station some Croats in Planian.

The position Daun had chosen was ideally suited to his cautious and defensive nature. The main position stretched from Pobortz Hill on the left flank across Przerovsky Hill and eventually on to Krzeczor Hill on the right flank. Both flanks are afforded some extra protection, the left with the Beczvarka Stream and on the right the village of Krzeczor and the Oak Wood situated a few hundred metres to the south of the village. Both Przerovsky Hill and Krzeczor Hill are 330m in height and dominate the Kaiser Strasse in the foothills and the plain rolling away northwards towards the Elbe. Marshal Daun would have a clear view of any Prussian troop movement. The northern slopes of the position would afford clear fields of fire, although in a few places the nature of the slope gives the attacker the brief respite of dead ground before the final ascent. The saddle between Przerovsky Hill and Krzeczor Hill, along with a steep-sided ravine cutting into the position near Bristvi and the valley to the east of Krzeczor, would help to break up any attack. The ground behind the main position slopes away to the south and is dead ground to anyone moving down the Kaiser Strasse. Daun would be able to move troops without being detected. The ridge gives the impression of running parallel with the Kaiser Strasse – this in fact is not the case. Pobortz on the left flank is three kilometres from the Kaiser Strasse as it leaves Planian running in a fairly straight line towards Kolin, but after six kilometres a spur juts out about 1km from Krzeczor Hill, reaching the Kaiser Strasse.

Had Daun been expecting to fight Frederick he almost certainly would have prepared the ground by constructing battery positions with breastworks and ditches, fortified the village of Krzeczor and exploited the defensive potential of the walled churchyard and the three-sided earthworks, known as 'The Swedish Fieldworks', constructed by Gustavus Adolphus during the Thirty Years War. The farm land over which the battle was fought is some of the most fertile arable land in Bohemia and with the growing season well under way, the eighteenth-century cereal crops of wheat and rye with their much longer stalks were sufficiently high to afford cover, most particularly for the Croats. For Frederick as he moved down the Kaiser Strasse and looked down the line of the hills forming Daun's position there was no obvious point from where an attack could be launched. A proper reconnaissance of the Austrian positions was going to be vital if any turning movement of Daun's right flank was to be successful.

FREDERICK'S FLANK MARCH

With the early morning mist still hugging the ground, Frederick and the lead elements of his army neared Planian. Major-General Beck, in Planian with some Croats, fired a few shots at the Prussians and then followed his orders by withdrawing to Radenin. Planian lies in a hollow and to get his bearings Frederick climbed to the top of the church tower. Unable to confirm the extent of the Austrian positions he descended and rejoined his troops as they made a right turn to push down the Kaiser Strasse. Lieutenant-General Hans Joachim von Zieten was leading the way with 50 squadrons of hussars and four battalions of infantry, pushing back the light troops of General of Cavalry Franz Leopold Nadasty, who had redeployed during the night to the right flank. Frederick was at the head of his army as it climbed out of the hollow and into the open countryside. To

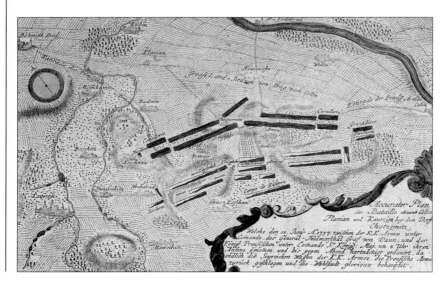

For its time this is quite an accurate map of the battle. Like the other maps it clearly shows the land being heavily cultivated. (MSW)

An engraving of the Battle by Muller. The Prussians in the foreground. Nadasty is supposedly at point B just to the left of the burning church and Daun is at A, to the right of the burning building on the left of the picture. (MSW)

Prussian infantry advance up Przerovsky Hill at Kolin. Despite numerous attacks they were unable to dislodge the Austrians. (Engraving after Menzel, PH)

his right, a few thousand paces away, was the ridge with the Austrian army while to his left the plain disappeared towards the Elbe. The bright sun and clear blue skies promised a glorious summer's day and Frederick could pick out more and more of the Austrian positions, but still he was unable to ascertain the full extent of Daun's dispositions. As Frederick moved down the Kaiser Strasse his army was sniped at by Croats using the high crops as cover, all the Prussian soldier's saw was a coat tail as a Croat moved to another position. Two and a half kilometres from Planian there was a wayside inn called 'Novi Mesto', near a hamlet of the same name, and it was here that Frederick called a halt. It was 10.30am when Frederick advanced his leading infantry regiments 300 paces towards the ridge and then called a halt, the sun was already making the day hot and having marched for four or five hours his troops were delighted with the opportunity to rest. The inn of Novi Mesto was of a good height and to get a better view of Daun's positions Frederick climbed to the top floor, with his generals.

While Frederick was halted at Novi Mesto, Daun had been observing his movements with interest. As yet the right wing of his position still rested on Przerovsky Hill, the rest of the ridge still being unguarded. This was beginning to be rectified with the deployment of the three Saxon Chevauxleger regiments in an extended line on the reverse slope

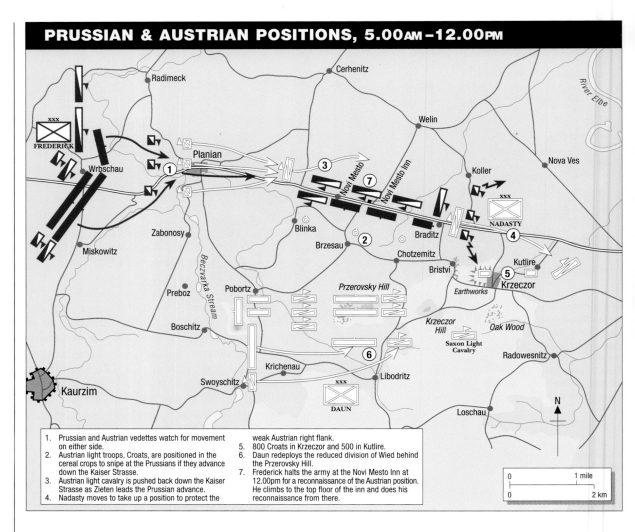

PRUSSIAN & AUSTRIAN POSITIONS, 5.00AM – 12.00PM

Radimeck
Cerhenitz
River Elbe
Welin
Nova Ves
FREDERICK
Koller
Wrbschau
Planian
Novi Mesto
Novi Mesto Inn
NADASTY
Zabonosy
Blinka
Bradiz
Miskowitz
Brzesau
Chotzemitz
Kutlire
Bristvi
Krzeczor
Preboz
Poborlz
Przerovsky Hill
Earthworks
Boschitz
Krzeczor Hill
Oak Wood
Saxon Light Cavalry
Radowesnitz
Krichenau
Libodritz
Kaurzim
Swoyschitz
DAUN
Loschau

N

1. Prussian and Austrian vedettes watch for movement on either side.
2. Austrian light troops, Croats, are positioned in the cereal crops to snipe at the Prussians if they advance down the Kaiser Strasse.
3. Austrian light cavalry is pushed back down the Kaiser Strasse as Zieten leads the Prussian advance.
4. Nadasty moves to take up a position to protect the weak Austrian right flank.
5. 800 Croats in Krzeczor and 500 in Kutlire.
6. Daun redeploys the reduced division of Wied behind the Przerovsky Hill.
7. Frederick halts the army at the Novi Mesto Inn at 12.00pm for a reconnaissance of the Austrian position. He climbs to the top floor of the inn and does his reconnaissance from there.

0   1 mile
0   2 km

Looking towards Krzeczor church with The 'Swedish' earthworks on the right, which remain impressive nearly 370 years after they were constructed. The Banalisten Croats defended the earthworks against the initial Prussian attacks. (Author)

THE INITIAL PRUSSIAN ATTACK

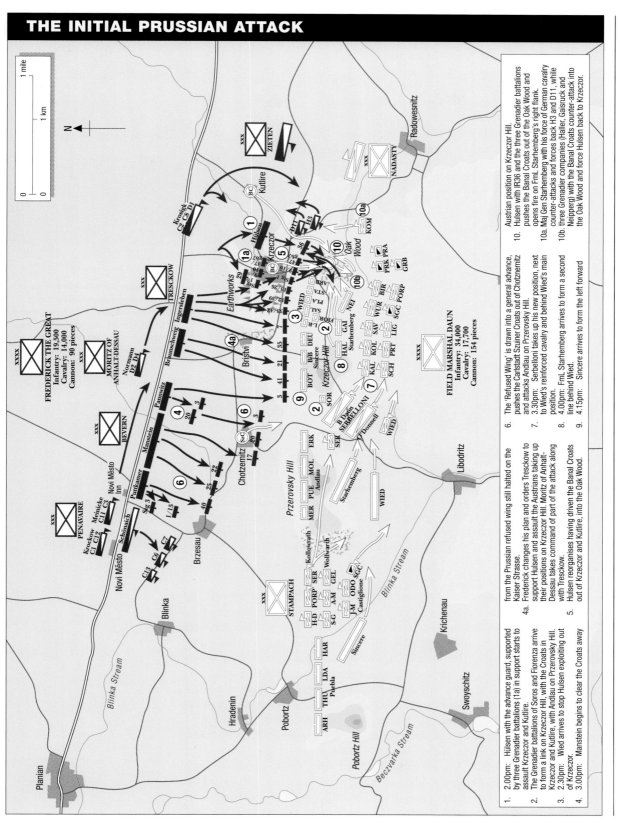

FREDERICK THE GREAT
Infantry: 19,500
Cavalry: 14,000
Cannon: 90 pieces

FIELD MARSHAL DAUN
Infantry: 34,000
Cavalry: 17,700
Cannon: 154 pieces

1. 2.00pm: Hülsen with the advance guard, supported by three Grenadier battalions (1a) in support starts to assault Krzeczor and Kutlire.

2. The Grenadier battalions of Soros and Fiorenza arrive to form a link on Krzeczor Hill, with the Croats in Krzeczor and Kutlire, with Andlau on Przerovsky Hill.

3. 2.30pm: Wied arrives to stop Hülsen exploiting out of Krzeczor.

4. 3.00pm: Manstein begins to clear the Croats away

from the Prussian refused wing still halted on the Kaiser Strasse.

4a. Frederick changes his plan and orders Tresckow to support Hülsen and assault the Austrians taking up their positions on Krzeczor Hill. Moritz of Anhalt-Dessau takes command of part of the attack along with Tresckow.

5. Hülsen reorganises having driven the Banal Croats out of Krzeczor and Kutlire, into the Oak Wood.

6. The 'Refused Wing' is drawn into a general advance, pushes the Carlstadt Szuiner Croats out of Chotznemitz and attacks Andlau on Przerovsky Hill.

7. 3.30pm: Serbelloni takes up his new position, next to Wied's reinforced cavalry and behind Wied's main position.

8. 4.00pm: FmL Starhemberg arrives to form a second line behind Wied.

9. 4.15pm: Sincere arrives to form the left forward

Austrian position on Krzeczor Hill.

10. Hülsen with IR36 and the three Grenadier battalions pushes the Banal Croats out of the Oak Wood and opens fire on FmL Starhemberg's right flank.

10a. Maj Gen Starhemberg with his force of German cavalry counter-attacks and forces back H3 and D11, while

10b. three Grenadier companies (Haller, Gaisruck and Neipperg) with the Banal Croats counter-attack into the Oak Wood and force Hulsen back to Krzeczor.

51

of Krzeczor Hill by Nadasty, who also placed 800 Croats with some light artillery, noisy 1-pdr and, from the reserve, 3-pdr cannon, in Krzeczor and finally 500 Croats in the village of Kutlire, about a kilometre, north east of Krzeczor. These deployments were to prove very fortunate. The closest troops to the main position on Nadasty's left flank were the *Kommandierten*, a mixed regular cavalry unit 1,000-strong, under the command of Major-General Johann Ludwig von Starhemberg.

Frederick from the top floor of the Novi Mesto inn was deciding what course of action to take. Although he did not know from experience what sort of commander Field Marshal Daun would prove to be, he was impressed with the position chosen. His generals were urging caution, but Frederick with the confidence of having turned the Austrians out of a good position at the Battle of Prague only six weeks earlier was confident of the ability of his army to do likewise again and in his own ability to direct them. His generals and men, however, were not so confident; the Austrians at Lobositz and Prague had proved that they were no longer a pushover. Any battle would be hard fought. Observing the ridge with his telescope Frederick would have been able to see that Krzeczor Hill was not occupied – this would be the place to strike. The plan formulating in his mind would see his army continuing it's march down the Kaiser Strasse and beyond the spur stretching out from the village of Krzeczor. They would then execute a right turn and march up on to Krzeczor Hill and roll up the Austrian right flank. The village of Krzeczor would consolidate this formation's right flank. The result of a successful attack here had the potential to be devastating for the Austrians for if Daun did not react with energy either to reinforce his right flank or withdraw to the south, they would be in danger of being rolled up and pushed into the Beczvarka stream and destroyed.

His mind made up and his plan formulated Frederick issued his orders to his generals in the inn. The first stage was for Zieten with 50 squadrons of hussars to push back the light cavalry of Nadasty, beyond the villages of Krzeczor and Kutlire and ensure they did not interfere with the execution of the attack. Major-General Joachim Dietrich von Hülsen would form an advance guard of three grenadier battalions, Kahlden, Möllendorf and Wangenheim, the infantry regiments IR29 (Schültze) and IR36 (Münchow), the 11th Dragoons (Stechow) and six cannon. Hülsen's force would deliver the blow. His task would be to prepare the way for the main army by advancing down the Kaiser Strasse and on passing the spur, he would, at a suitable point, execute a right turn and screened from the Austrian position advance up on to the high ground by way of Krzeczor and secure the ground for deployment. Frederick, not crediting his enemy with the foresight to put troops in Krzeczor, expected no opposition. The main army would be split into

The walled church at Krzeczor. The trees are young and it is difficult to say if there were any trees on the day of battle. The church was defended by Banalisten Croats. (Author)

two forces, the left wing following behind Hülsen would be Lieutenant-General von Pennavaire's powerful cavalry wing of Krosigk, Normann, Meinicke and Krockow – a total of six cuirassier and three dragoon regiments and the eight infantry battalions of Lieutenant-Général von Tresckow's command. The right wing of the army under Lieutenant-General von Bevern, 14 battalions of infantry, the three remaining grenadier battalions and Major-General von Schönaich's four cavalry regiments would be refused on the Kaiser Strasse to fix the attention of Daun and the Austrians up on the ridge. Frederick anticipated the Austrians accommodating his plan by doing nothing to interfere with the movements of his army.

HÜLSEN ADVANCES

Field Marshal Daun was up on the ridge with his suite; his soldiers resting, but like their commander puzzled by the Prussian lack of activity. The sun was high in the sky and the glorious summer's day was hot when Daun called a council of war. One of those present was Major Franz Vettez of the regiment Erzherzog Karl, who had a sharp mind and Daun made a point of seeking his opinion. Vettez was convinced that a battle was almost certain and the most likely point of attack would be over towards Krzeczor, with Frederick trying to roll up the right flank. While Daun was watching the scene on the Kaiser Strasse he gave word that Wied with the reserve was to move his division and take post behind the command of Lieutenant-General Johann Winulph von Starhemberg on Przerovsky Hill. It was soon after this order was dispatched that there was activity in the Prussian camp. The sun glinted on the thousands of musket barrels and there was a flash as the order was given to fix bayonets. Soon afterwards at 1.30pm the Prussian army was on the move. Zieten, pushing ahead as ordered, made contact with Nadasty and drove the Austrian light cavalry back as had been planned. They also came under fire from the light artillery pieces of the Croats in Krzeczor, but continued with their task. Hülsen, marching up the Kaiser Strasse, was just passing the inn of 'U slunce' (At the Sun) in Braditz when he too came under fire from the Croats in Krzeczor. Hülsen's casualties were minimal, but this was an unexpected surprise. Krzeczor was occupied and Frederick must have begun to realise that not only would Hülsen now have a fight on his hands, but that he himself was facing a far more wily adversary than expected in Marshal Daun.

Hülsen turned to his right and formed his command for an attack on Krzeczor. At 2.00pm he launched his attack, supported by his artillery, advancing up the spur from the Kaiser Strasse and up the valley between Krzeczor and Kutlire. At the same time Frederick ordered the three remaining grenadier battalions to advance diagonally up the slope from Braditz to support the attack on Krzeczor. Frederick halted his army once again to await the outcome. Daun, who had been observing the deployments in silence, is

A small Austrian field piece, the 3-pdr cannon. Based on the model of 1718 the 3-pdr fired a shot about the size of a tennis ball. The Croats were issued with 1-pdr, 2-pdr and 2.5-pdr pieces which were very ineffective and along with the 3-pdr soon passed out of use. (Print after Ottenfeld/PH)

Field Marshal Daun, with his staff on Przerovsky Hill, observes the movement of the Prussian army on the Kaiser Strasse. His position on the ridge line made his command and control much easier and therefore gave him a decision-making advantage over Frederick. (Adam Hook)

reputed to have remarked, 'My God, I think the King is going to lose today!' Musketry and light artillery fire crackled and boomed as the Banalisten Croats, within the walled churchyard and the earthworks inflicted severe casualties on the Prussians. Hülsen, a dogged and determined commander, nevertheless pressed the attack home and very soon the Croats were executing a fighting withdrawal through the village. Within half an hour Hülsen had fought through Krzeczor and was on the open ground to the south of the village, with the Banalisten Croats heading for the Oak Wood. The Prussians however were not able to push on for, as they emerged from the village for the first time, they were beaten back by some of Nadasty's hussars.

While Hülsen had been fighting his way through the village, Nadasty and Zieten had in the meantime been fighting their own private battle. Nadasty had sent forward four detachments of hussars and these troops had been niggling away at Zieten since the early morning when they had been deployed near Planian. They had endured two hours of artillery fire and then fallen back to form a screen across the Kaiser Strasse near the inn of U slunce. When the Prussian advance had begun, they skirmished with Zieten's hussars in the vicinity of Kutlire and then fell back over the Krzeczor–Kutlire valley and joined the main body of Nadasty on the right. It is now that Nadasty and Zieten become embroiled in the events at Krzeczor. The Banalisten Croats were vulnerable as they retreated back to the Oak Wood and were about to be charged by the Zieten Hussars when the Austrian Kaiser Hussars came to

their rescue with a timely counter-charge. Safely in the Oak Wood the Croats opened up a concentrated fire on the Prussian hussars and with Nadasty organising a more concerted counter-attack the Prussians were beaten back into the village. For the remainder of the battle Zieten and Nadasty fought out various indecisive combats on the axis Krzeczor-Radowesnitz, with neither side being able to gain an advantage.

Daun, seeing the attack developing on his right flank, immediately ordered Major Soro with four companies and Lieutenant-Colonel Marquis Fiorenza with six companies of grenadiers and four cannon to cover the right flank of the army until other regiments arrived to support them. Soro's grenadier battalion formed up on Krzeczor Hill between Chotzemitz and Bristvi, while Fiorenza strode out with his command and deployed towards Krzeczor village. This meagre line was all that linked the main body of the Austrian army with Nadasty's wing. Fiorenza's grenadiers and artillery were soon engaged in a fire fight with Hülsen as he emerged again from Krzeczor with his infantry and supporting artillery of 20 guns. The support promised by Daun was not long in coming. Lieutenant-General Heinrich Karl Wied, who was already on the move with his weakened command of six battalions of infantry and two cavalry regiments, was now ordered to take position as the first line on the right wing with the greatest possible speed. The sun was burning in the sky as Wied's troops, raising a cloud of dust and sweating from their exertions, marched to occupy their new ground – they would be in position by 3.30pm. Word had also been sent for 12 guns of the artillery reserve to move to the south-west of Krzeczor and support Wied. The artillery moved with such energy that some of the guns arrived before the lead elements of Wied's battalions. They immediately started a counter-battery duel with Hülsen's battery and quickly gained the upper hand.

Frederick kept his army halted until 3.00pm, when he gave the order for the army to deploy in their current position and prepare to advance against the Austrians. The Prussian regiments executed a right turn to bring themselves into a continuous line of battle, ready to advance. Prince Moritz of Anhalt-Dessau, the army second in command, understood the original plan only too well and realising that the

Austrian dragoons come under artillery fire at Kolin. The Austrian cavalry were particulary cool under fire at Kolin, suffering many casualties yet remaining at their post. (ASKB)

Prussians needed to march a further 2km along the Kaiser Strasse before launching their assault, remonstrated with Frederick and had to be ordered to obey three times. He did eventually, muttering 'and now the battle is lost'. It is likely that Frederick had seen the dust cloud caused by Wied and guessing that Daun was reinforcing his right realised he urgently had to seize the ridge.

TRESCKOW'S ASSAULT ON KRZECZOR HILL

Frederick's new plan was for Lieutenant-General Tresckow with the eight battalions of his command and one battalion of IR3 (Anhalt) to advance up the forward slopes of Krzeczor Hill and come up on the right flank of the three grenadier battalions sent to support Hülsen. For the moment the remainder of his army, the right wing, would be refused. Or so he thought. Further back down the line, however, Bevern's infantry were being plagued by Croats, sniping at them from the cover provided by the tall cereal crops. Frustrated watching his men stand idly by whilst taking casualties Major-General Christoph von Manstein was delighted when one of Frederick's adjutants, the Marquis de Varenne rode past and shouted out that the Croats must be driven away. A tough and experienced soldier who had seen many years in the service of Russia, Manstein was reluctant to be diverted from his orders, to support the left wing of the army when the time came. Varenne citing royal authority urged Manstein to act and even asked Anhalt-Dessau to order Manstein to comply. With some misgiving Manstein turned to the nearest troops, the second battalion of IR20 (Bornstedt) from the brigade of Pannwitz, and ordered them to clear the Croats. In their enthusiasm to deal with the irritating Croats they ventured too far and came under heavy fire from more Croats in the village of Chotzemitz and cannon on Przerovsky Hill. Before long the men of the first battalion IR20 waded into the fields, without orders, to support their comrades, taking with them the remaining battalion of IR3. Soon all three battalions evicted the Croats

The continuation of the 'Swedish fieldworks' just north of the church. These earthworks were the remains of fortifications constructed by the troops of Swedish King Gustavus Adolphus during the Thirty Years War over 100 years before. (Author)

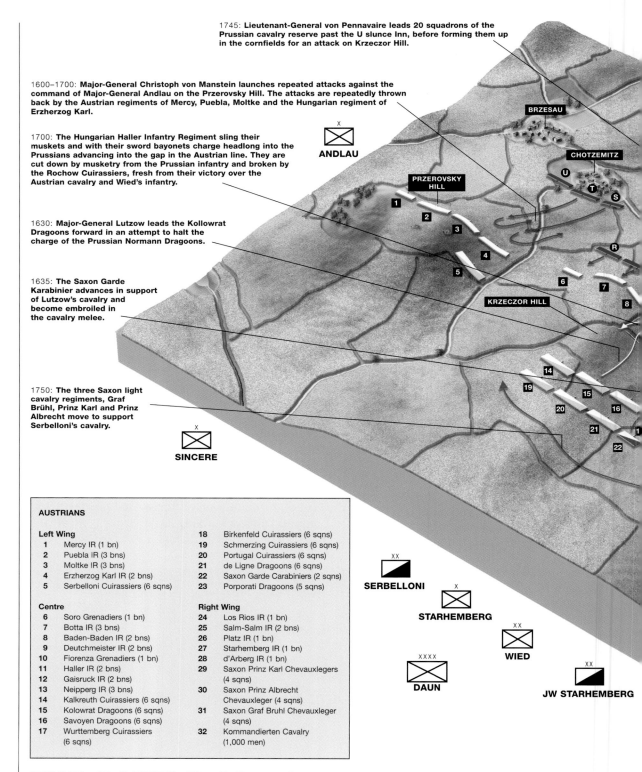

1745: Lieutenant-General von Pennavaire leads 20 squadrons of the Prussian cavalry reserve past the U slunce Inn, before forming them up in the cornfields for an attack on Krzeczor Hill.

1600–1700: Major-General Christoph von Manstein launches repeated attacks against the command of Major-General Andlau on the Przerovsky Hill. The attacks are repeatedly thrown back by the Austrian regiments of Mercy, Puebla, Moltke and the Hungarian regiment of Erzherzog Karl.

1700: The Hungarian Haller Infantry Regiment sling their muskets and with their sword bayonets charge headlong into the Prussians advancing into the gap in the Austrian line. They are cut down by musketry from the Prussian infantry and broken by the Rochow Cuirassiers, fresh from their victory over the Austrian cavalry and Wied's infantry.

1630: Major-General Lutzow leads the Kollowrat Dragoons forward in an attempt to halt the charge of the Prussian Normann Dragoons.

1635: The Saxon Garde Karabinier advances in support of Lutzow's cavalry and become embroiled in the cavalry melee.

1750: The three Saxon light cavalry regiments, Graf Brühl, Prinz Karl and Prinz Albrecht move to support Serbelloni's cavalry.

ANDLAU

BRZESAU

CHOTZEMITZ

PRZEROVSKY HILL

KRZECZOR HILL

SINCERE

SERBELLONI

STARHEMBERG

WIED

DAUN

JW STARHEMBERG

AUSTRIANS

Left Wing
1   Mercy IR (1 bn)
2   Puebla IR (3 bns)
3   Moltke IR (3 bns)
4   Erzherzog Karl IR (2 bns)
5   Serbelloni Cuirassiers (6 sqns)

Centre
6   Soro Grenadiers (1 bn)
7   Botta IR (3 bns)
8   Baden-Baden IR (2 bns)
9   Deutchmeister IR (2 bns)
10 Fiorenza Grenadiers (1 bn)
11 Haller IR (2 bns)
12 Gaisruck IR (2 bns)
13 Neipperg IR (3 bns)
14 Kalkreuth Cuirassiers (6 sqns)
15 Kolowrat Dragoons (6 sqns)
16 Savoyen Dragoons (6 sqns)
17 Wurttemberg Cuirassiers (6 sqns)

18 Birkenfeld Cuirassiers (6 sqns)
19 Schmerzing Cuirassiers (6 sqns)
20 Portugal Cuirassiers (6 sqns)
21 de Ligne Dragoons (6 sqns)
22 Saxon Garde Carabiniers (2 sqns)
23 Porporati Dragoons (5 sqns)

Right Wing
24 Los Rios IR (1 bn)
25 Salm-Salm IR (2 bns)
26 Platz IR (1 bn)
27 Starhemberg IR (1 bn)
28 d'Arberg IR (1 bn)
29 Saxon Prinz Karl Chevauxlegers (4 sqns)
30 Saxon Prinz Albrecht Chevauxleger (4 sqns)
31 Saxon Graf Bruhl Chevauxleger (4 sqns)
32 Kommandierten Cavalry (1,000 men)

THE BATTLE OF KOLIN

18th June 1757, viewed from the south-east showing the charge of Major-General von Krosigk's cavalry and the destruction of Lieutenant-General Wied's infantry.

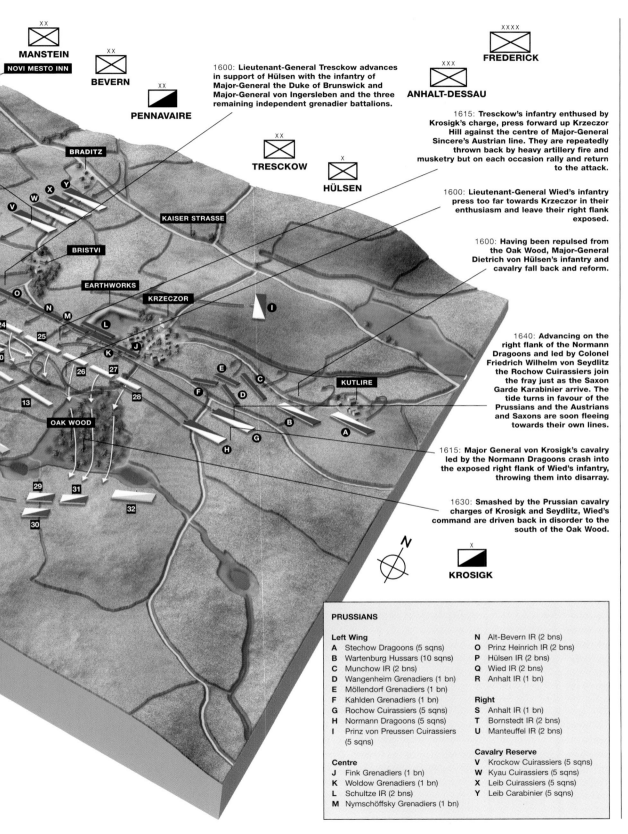

MANSTEIN

NOVI MESTO INN

BEVERN

PENNAVAIRE

FREDERICK

ANHALT-DESSAU

1600: Lieutenant-General Tresckow advances in support of Hülsen with the infantry of Major-General the Duke of Brunswick and Major-General von Ingersleben and the three remaining independent grenadier battalions.

BRADITZ

TRESCKOW

HÜLSEN

1615: Tresckow's infantry enthused by Krosigk's charge, press forward up Krzeczor Hill against the centre of Major-General Sincere's Austrian line. They are repeatedly thrown back by heavy artillery fire and musketry but on each occasion rally and return to the attack.

KAISER STRASSE

1600: Lieutenant-General Wied's infantry press too far towards Krzeczor in their enthusiasm and leave their right flank exposed.

BRISTVI

1600: Having been repulsed from the Oak Wood, Major-General Dietrich von Hülsen's infantry and cavalry fall back and reform.

EARTHWORKS

KRZECZOR

1640: Advancing on the right flank of the Normann Dragoons and led by Colonel Friedrich Wilhelm von Seydlitz the Rochow Cuirassiers join the fray just as the Saxon Garde Karabinier arrive. The tide turns in favour of the Prussians and the Austrians and Saxons are soon fleeing towards their own lines.

KUTLIRE

OAK WOOD

1615: Major General von Krosigk's cavalry led by the Normann Dragoons crash into the exposed right flank of Wied's infantry, throwing them into disarray.

1630: Smashed by the Prussian cavalry charges of Krosigk and Seydlitz, Wied's command are driven back in disorder to the south of the Oak Wood.

KROSIGK

PRUSSIANS

Left Wing

A Stechow Dragoons (5 sqns)
B Wartenburg Hussars (10 sqns)
C Munchow IR (2 bns)
D Wangenheim Grenadiers (1 bn)
E Möllendorf Grenadiers (1 bn)
F Kahlden Grenadiers (1 bn)
G Rochow Cuirassiers (5 sqns)
H Normann Dragoons (5 sqns)
I Prinz von Preussen Cuirassiers (5 sqns)

Centre

J Fink Grenadiers (1 bn)
K Woldow Grenadiers (1 bn)
L Schultze IR (2 bns)
M Nymschöffsky Grenadiers (1 bn)
N Alt-Bevern IR (2 bns)
O Prinz Heinrich IR (2 bns)
P Hülsen IR (2 bns)
Q Wied IR (2 bns)
R Anhalt IR (1 bn)

Right

S Anhalt IR (1 bn)
T Bornstedt IR (2 bns)
U Manteuffel IR (2 bns)

Cavalry Reserve

V Krockow Cuirassiers (5 sqns)
W Kyau Cuirassiers (5 sqns)
X Leib Cuirassiers (5 sqns)
Y Leib Carabinier (5 sqns)

from Chotzemitz and began a series of frontal assaults on Przerovsky Hill.

Hülsen was now engaged in a fire fight with his back against the southern edge of Krzeczor village, with Tresckow advancing to support him and the supposedly uncommitted right wing being drawn into an attack on Chotzemitz and ultimately Przerovsky Hill. What of the Austrians? Daun had ordered Starhemberg and Sincere to move east and support Wied, forming a continuous line along the ridge. He also ordered General of Cavalry Serbelloni to move his command to give immediate support to Wied. Serbelloni was an arrogant member of the Milanese aristocracy and was renowned for his sluggishness, as his performance during Frederick's invasion of Bohemia in April testified. On this occasion, however, he acted with urgency and led his command off to the right with almost reckless speed. The Carabinier squadron of the Schmerzing Cuirassiers crashed into a ravine, putting the majority of them out of action. Serbelloni's first position was between the two grenadier battalions. At the same time three regiments from General of Cavalry Stampach's command, the Serbelloni Cuirassiers, Saxon Garde Carabiniers and Porporati Dragoons, were detached to support the right and come under Serbelloni's command. The Serbelloni Cuirassiers were assigned to support Andlau on Przerovsky Hill, while the Saxon Garde Carabinier and the Porporati Dragoons were attached to the cavalry of Wied's Division. With the battle raging around Krzeczor and Tresckow advancing to support Hülsen, Starhemberg was ordered to provide a second line on Krzeczor Hill. His regiments, Neipperg, Gaisruck and Haller were in position by 4.00pm and had all taken casualties from artillery fire as they marched to form the second line. The most important reinforcements of all however were still to arrive, the strong division of Lieutenant-General Claudius von Sincere was coming from Pobortz Hill, marching with a sense of urgency. While all these redeployments were happening, at 3.30pm Tresckow was advancing as ordered up the slopes of Krzeczor Hill, with his nine battalions deployed in two lines. Lieutenant Prittwitz of IR7 (Alt-Bevern), was delighted to be on the move again, but very soon 'we began to feel the effect of the enemy artillery fire … shot and shell passed clear over our heads, more than enough also crashed into our ranks to smash large numbers of our men.' The two lines of Tresckow's command advanced solidly through the neck-high corn, forming a single line as they advanced. On reaching the crest of the hill they were greeted with a hail of canister that cut swathes through the Prussian line. Hülsen's artillery meanwhile was putting down intense fire on Serbelloni's exposed cavalry, and for once the Austrians were well served by Serbelloni's arrogance and inflexible attitude as he kept his cavalry to the task of holding the line. To help the situation Serbelloni rotated his regiments in the front line with those

A romantic view of the battle. Marshal Daun is in the foreground with General Nadasty at his side. (MSW)

from the second, ensuring that his regiments received some relief from the fire. While Serbelloni's cavalrymen patiently endured the telling artillery fire Starhemberg and Sincere were taking up their positions. The leading elements of Sincere's division arrived just as Tresckow crested the hill with his nine battalions and were immediately involved in a fierce musketry duel with the Prussian infantry. Both sides suffered tremendous casualties, the Prussian infantry firing regimental volleys. Tresckow was unable to advance any further for although the Fiorenza grenadier battalion and the supporting lead battalion were shot through, with Lieutenant-Colonel Fiorenza killed, the smoke lifted to reveal the remainder of Sincere's Division arriving 'in excellent order and drawn up shoulder to shoulder'. By 4.15pm his three regiments, Botta, Baden-Baden and Deutschmeister were in position to the left of Wied in the first line on Krzeczor Hill. Daun had now achieved a solid front across Przerovsky Hill and Krzeczor Hill. Having been replaced by Sincere, Serbelloni moved his cavalry to form a third line behind Starhemberg. The forward regiments of Wied and Sincere held firm and repeatedly threw back Tresckow's line. The Prussians took shelter in the sunken road running from Krzeczor via Bristvi to Chotzemitz and at times found themselves at the very bottom of the hill. Again and again Tresckow and his officers rallied their troops and returned to the attack.

At the same time that Starhemberg was arriving to form a second line behind Wied, two Prussian grenadier battalions of Hülsen's command, Mollendorf and Wangenheim, and IR36 managed to break into the Oak Wood; entering from the eastern edge, they had a fierce fight with the Croats before finally scattering and driving them southwards out of the wood. The Prussian infantry then proceeded to open fire on the Austrians of Starhemberg. The wood was not to remain

The view of Krzeczor church the Prussian grenadier battalion 9/10 (Mollendorf) would have had as they advanced towards the village. (Author)

The Austrian Infantry Regiment Botta repel the charge of the Normann Dragoons. Daun's right flank had collapsed after 12 of his 18 battalions had been ridden down by Krosigk's charge. The steadfastness of IR Botta enabled the Austrians on the right flank to gather their wits and snatch away from Frederick a battle-winning position. (Adam Hook)

in Prussian hands for long. Almost immediately Nadasty rallied the Croats and launched them back into the fray. Major-General J. Ludwig Starhemberg at the same time covered the vulnerable right flank of the Croats by advancing with his 1,000 Kommandierten cavalry against the 11th Prussian Dragoons and 3rd Hussars (Wartenberg), throwing them back in confusion towards Kutlire. As LtGen Starhemberg arrived he gathered together a grenadier company from each of his regiments and ordered them to clear the wood. They advanced towards the Oak Wood and on arriving at the western edge opened up a regular platoon fire. Eventually the Prussians gave way, meeting as they fled three cannon being brought up to lend support to their cause, but at the sight of the Austrians the gunners cut their traces and abandoned the guns.

The Destruction of Wied's Division

Events were going well for Daun. His position on Krzeczor Hill and Przerovsky Hill was secure and most importantly he had managed to get Frederick to change his plans. The Prussians were still formidable opponents though and the first crisis for Daun was about to descend on his right flank. Flushed with the success of throwing the Prussians out of the Oak Wood, Wied's Division, in all likelihood without his orders, advanced towards Krzeczor village, losing the relative protection on their right flank of the Oak Wood. Major-General Christian Siegfried von Krosigk had been following behind Hülsen with his command of the left wing cavalry, 2nd Cuirassiers (Prinz von Preussen), 8th Cuirassiers (Rochow) and 1st Dragoons (Normann), and the vulnerability of Wied's Division did not escape his notice. He had already sent 2nd Cuirassiers around to the north of Krzeczor and with his two remaining regiments launched them at the exposed right flank of Wied. The first line, made up of 1st Dragoons, crashed into the Austrian infantry. The battalions of d'Arberg and Starhemberg were swiftly overwhelmed and it was only after disaster had befallen them that the battalion of Platz realised their mistake in thinking the cuirassiers were friendly forces. Their fate was the same as the Prussian troopers cut and slashed their way through the unfortunate battalion. During this melee Krosigk was mortally wounded and thrown from his horse. The grenadier battalions 13/26 (Fink), 33/42 (Nymschöfsky) and 12/39 (Waldow) of Treskow's left wing and Hulsen's IR 29 now advanced into the fray. The three remaining battalions of Wied's command, a battalion of Los Rios and two battalions of Salm-Salm, fled at the sight of the lowered Prussian bayonets and the marauding Prussian cavalry to their right. The Austrian right flank was in a perilous situation and Major-General Lützow led the Kolowrat Dragoons through the intervals of Starhemberg's division and on into the swirling mass of men. Lützow was killed as 1st Prussian Dragoons hit the Kolowrat Dragoons hard in their flank. The young colonel of 8th Cuirassiers, Colonel Friedrich Wilhelm von Seydlitz,

An interpretation of the Hungarian Infantry Regiment Haller having left their place in Starhemberg's line and becoming embroiled in Wied's struggle with Krosigk's cavalry. (MSW)

ABOVE **A typical Prussian curassier sword or 'Kurassierdegen' for troopers. This type is of 1732. (PM)**

LEFT **Detail of the basket of the cuirassier sword. (PM)**

was a little way behind the 1st Dragoons, but as he reached the southern edge of Krzeczor he led his regiment into the melee, on the right flank of the Normann Dragoons. The Saxon Garde Carabinier had just arrived to support the Kolowrat Dragoons. With the Prussians reinforced by Seydlitz's cavalrymen the tide turned in their favour and soon the Austrians and Saxons were fleeing towards their own lines. The battalions on Sincere's right were next to feel the pressure with Wied's line swept away, Hülsen and Tresckow advancing to their front and Prussian and friendly cavalrymen swirling around their flank. The regiments of Deutschmeister and Baden-Baden gave way, when the Normann Dragoons got in amongst them. The time was now close to 5.00pm and to add to the chaos on the right, the Hungarian regiment of Haller slung their muskets, drew their swords and charged the Prussians who were advancing into the gap. Their fate was the same as that of Wied's battalions; they were cut down by musketry from the well-drilled Prussian battalions and finally broken by the victorious cuirassiers under Seydlitz, who were completing their successful charge.

The battle was so nearly won for Frederick: Daun's right flank had collapsed; Wied's division was in total disarray; Sincere had lost two out of his three regiments and Starhemberg one of his. Orders were now given for the army to retreat, although there is some question as to who issued them. It is likely that the order came from a general on the right who had lost his nerve and issued the order in the name of Marshal Daun. The commander's coolness in action was well known and it is unlikely he would have panicked in such a way; he did however remind his staff that Suchdol was the rallying point after any withdrawal. This reminder was unwise but the damage was done. The artillery train began to move and three cavalry regiments broke off an attack. It is unlikely that the Austrians would have been able to make a clean break and withdraw and so the majority of local commanders got on with fighting the battle.

All was not yet lost for Daun on the right flank. The regiment Salm-Salm was being rallied by their temporary commander Major Maximillian Prince zu Salm-Salm. They formed up in the gap left by Regiment Haller, joining the two other regiments of Starhemberg's division, Gaisruck and Neipperg. It fell once again to Serbelloni's cavalry to form part of the first line facing the Prussians, and again they performed their task well, under heavy fire. The greatest danger however was on the western edge of Krzeczor Hill where the integrity of Daun's line was dependent on Sincere's sole remaining regiment, that of Botta. The regiment had held firm, firing controlled volleys and beating back the Prussian attacks to their front. They had however expended all their ammunition. Once again the Prussians advanced and this time regiment Botta, having had no time to redistribute ammunition, had to force them back at bayonet point. It seemed that all their efforts were to be in vain as the victorious 1st Prussian Dragoons appeared through the smoke and dust on their right flank and formed up to charge the **65** isolated regiment. While the Prussian dragoons organised themselves for the charge, the officers of Botta wheeled the regiment back by its right, forming an eastward-facing front. They redistributed ammunition whilst the remnants of Baden-Baden and Deutschmeister rallied to their right. For once the Prussian obsession with precision let them down; taking too long to re-form, they charged but were met with a volley and were subsequently chased away by some Saxon Chevauxleger.

'DOGS, DO YOU WISH TO LIVE FOREVER?'

In front of Przerovsky Hill the Prussians under Manstein had eventually been able to drive out the two battalions of Szluiner Croats defending Chotzemitz. The Croats withdrew towards their own lines, but became caught in the crossfire and were effectively shot down by their own side, as the regiments on Przerovsky Hill beat back the advancing Prussians who were following closely behind. In the end the Prussians were beaten back, recoiling with heavy losses to the southern edge of Chotzemitz. As they rallied the IR17 (Manteuffel) joined them on their right. The Prussians readied themselves and the five battalions then advanced up the steep slopes of Przerovsky Hill once again. Again the eight white-coated Austrian

LEFT **An original cartridge bag belonging to the Dragoon Regiment No.5 (Anspach-Bayreuth). This regiment was not at Kolin but is famous for their charge at Hohenfriedberg in 1745.**

BELOW **This pistol (model 1731) was used by the Prussian cuirassiers and dragoons. (PM)**

battalions of regiments Mercy, Puebla, Moltke and Erzherzog Karl, supported by the Soro Grenadier Battalion, beat back the Prussians. By 3.30pm two further determined attacks on Przerovsky Hill had been thrown back in confusion. Frederick's attention was concentrated on the attacks on Przerovsky Hill for most of the battle and during the afternoon he became increasingly frustrated by the attacks' lack of success. On one occasion he drew his sword and put himself at the head of a battalion of IR3 and to the beat of the *Strumstreich* he led them forwards. He was followed by scarcely 40 men, who fled when a cannon shot landed close to them. Frederick, unaware of this, rode towards the Austrian artillery and only stopped when his adjutant Grant asked him if he intended to capture the battery single

Frederick, despairing of the unsuccessful attacks on Przerovsky Hill, set off to attack the Hill thinking the men of IR3 were following him. He realises this is not the case when his ADC Grant rides up and asks. 'Sire! Will you attack the battery on your own?' (Print after Richard Knotel)

handed. It is highly likely that it was as a result of this humiliation that he is said to have shouted 'Dogs, do you wish to live forever?'

During the afternoon Daun gave orders for the division of Lieutenant-General Puebla, which to this point had not been involved in the battle, to move by detachments to the east and link up with Andlau on Przerovsky Hill. The other command as yet not involved was the cavalry wing of General of Cavalry Karl von Stampach. By 5.00pm the struggle on the right flank was at a critical stage and Daun issued another order, this time to Stampach, to advance and fall on the Prussian right wing. Stampach led his four cavalry regiments, the Gelhay and Alt-Modena Cuirassiers with the Hesse-Darmstadt and Saxe-Gotha Dragoons out towards the Prussians near Brzesau. The first objective of the advance was the Prussian cavalry commanded by Major-General Schönaich. Stampach decided to drive them in and then turn his attention to the Prussian battalions of the right wing under Lieutenant-General the Duke of Brunswick-Bevern. The Prussians frustrated Stampach's plans however. First Schönaich shifted his 18 squadrons of cavalry from a line Brzesau–Blinka to one Brzesau–Novi Mesto, making them much more difficult to turn. Secondly the Prussian infantry advanced aggressively and this was enough for Stampach to disengage and withdraw behind Puebla, forming up in his left rear. There was one bright point in this gloomy episode when the Hesse-Darmstadt Dragoons, held to their course by their commander the Count D'Ayasasa, charged into the first battalion of IR15, the Leibgarde Battalion. With the red-coated dragoons in amongst them there was little hope for the guardsmen and having destroyed the battalion to their satisfaction, capturing the two battalion guns and leaving the guardsmen scattered on the ground amongst the wheat the Hesse-Darmstadt Dragoons regained their lines with glory to their name. All was not as it seemed, for no sooner had the Austrian cavalry departed than the tough commanding officer Colonel Tauentzien and the survivors of the battalion picked themselves up, re-formed and marched off with drums and fifes playing.

Pennavaire's charge

Meanwhile the dramatic events on the Krzeczor continued to unfold. At around 5.30pm the Prussians began to lose the initiative gained by Krosigk's charge with the Austrians beginning to re-form either side of the gap on the Krzeczor Hill. The Prussian infantry were hot and tired after their exertions so far on this summers day and so it fell to Lieutenant-General Peter von Pennavaire with his four glorious cuirassier regiments to finish off the equally tired Austrian infantry on the heights. Towards 5.45pm Pennaviare led the 20 squadrons of 1st (Krockow), 3rd (Leibregiment), 11th (Leib Carabinier) and 12th (Kyau) Cuirassiers past the U slunce Inn, through the cornfields and on up the slopes of Krzeczor Hill, past Bristvi. It was an awe-inspiring sight for soldiers of both sides, and also a very inviting target for the Austrian artillery and the refugee Croats lurking in the sunken roads around Chotzemitz, who fired into the horsemen's right flank as they rode past. As he neared the crest Pennavaire deployed the 1st and 12th regiments in the first line and the 3rd and 11th in echelon behind. Pennavaire gave the order for the regiments to attack the three Austrian cuirassier regiments, Schmerzing, Portugal and Kalckreuth sent by Serbelloni to meet

Alou! With pluck
We are going to fight:
Our Queen Theresa
Is watching us.
(M. Ales/Author's collection)

A charming pen and ink sketch of Austrian dragoons at Leuthen. (M. Ales/Author's collection)

them. The two masses of horsemen thundered towards each other, both sides bracing themselves for the impact. They had closed to about 150 yards when quite inexplicably the Austrian horse veered to one side and made off back behind their own lines. The Prussian horsemen were amazed by this, but what they did not know was that a courier had arrived with the false order for the regiments to break off their attack and fall back in good order. Pennavaire riding his luck used the impetus of the movement to wheel his command to the left and bear down on the regiments of Gaisruck and the remnants of Salm-Salm – the left flank of Starhemberg's command. Fortune however favoured the Austrian line, for the Prussian cavalry was spent, they halted 20 paces away from the line of white coats and fired their pistols, they received a volley from Gaisruck and Salm-Salm and were in the process of retiring when they were attacked by successive waves of Austrian cavalry. The three Saxon chevauxleger regiments of Graf Brühl, Prinz Karl and Prinz Albert closely followed by the Kolowrat Dragoons, Savoyen Dragoons, the Birkenfeld Cuirassiers and the Saxon Garde Carabiniers crashed into the right flank of Pennavaire's static command. The Prussian cavalry's situation became more desperate when Major-General Starhemberg with his Kommandierten cavalry burst into their left flank from the direction of the Oak Wood. This was too much for the Prussian cuirassiers, who gave way and set off for the safety of the Kaiser Strasse in the wildest of disorder with the Austrian cavalry close behind, heedless of the cries of not only their officers but also of Frederick to rally. Another disaster was about to befall the Prussian cavalry arm when the 2nd Cuirassiers of Krosigk's old brigade, having made their way around the north of Krzeczor, arrived on the left flank of Tresckow's infantry. They were led through the intervals in the Prussian line by Moritz of Anhalt-Dessau and into an attack on the Austrian line of Starhemberg. It was another charge doomed to failure; as the unsupported cuirassiers closed on the white line of Austrian infantry they were met with a hail of canister and controlled volley fire. Shattered they

Chotzemitz lies in the middle distance with Brzesau in the distance. This was the ground covered by Frederick's supposed refused right wing and where Frederick spent most of the battle. Prussian IR 3 advanced across the immediate foreground helping to clear Croats from the vicinity of Chotzemitz. Between the two villages in the middle distance were three regiments of Bevern, IR22, 25 and 40. (Author's collection)

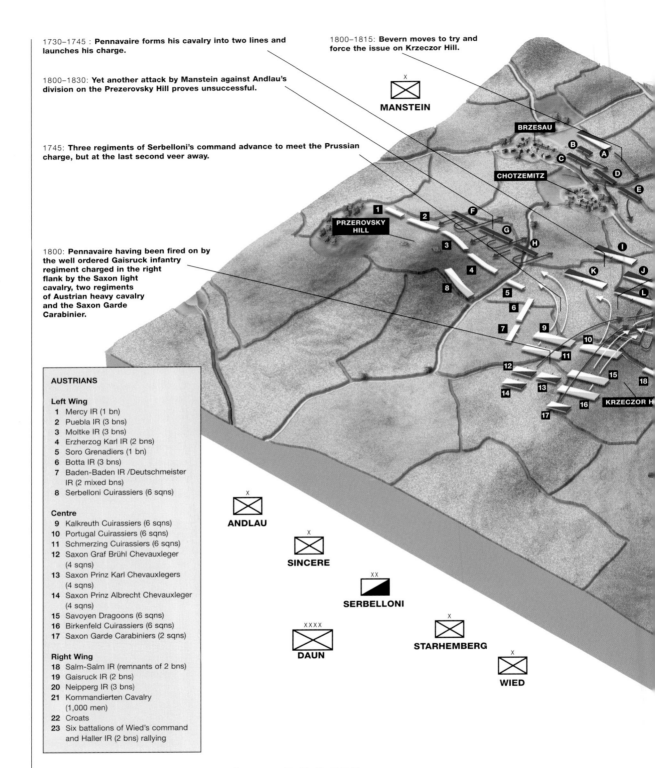

1730–1745 : Pennavaire forms his cavalry into two lines and launches his charge.

1800–1815: Bevern moves to try and force the issue on Krzeczor Hill.

1800–1830: Yet another attack by Manstein against Andlau's division on the Prezerovsky Hill proves unsuccessful.

1745: Three regiments of Serbelloni's command advance to meet the Prussian charge, but at the last second veer away.

1800: Pennavaire having been fired on by the well ordered Gaisruck infantry regiment charged in the right flank by the Saxon light cavalry, two regiments of Austrian heavy cavalry and the Saxon Garde Carabinier.

MANSTEIN

BRZESAU

CHOTZEMITZ

PRZEROVSKY HILL

KRZECZOR H

ANDLAU

SINCERE

SERBELLONI

DAUN

STARHEMBERG

WIED

AUSTRIANS

Left Wing
1 Mercy IR (1 bn)
2 Puebla IR (3 bns)
3 Moltke IR (3 bns)
4 Erzherzog Karl IR (2 bns)
5 Soro Grenadiers (1 bn)
6 Botta IR (3 bns)
7 Baden-Baden IR /Deutschmeister IR (2 mixed bns)
8 Serbelloni Cuirassiers (6 sqns)

Centre
9 Kalkreuth Cuirassiers (6 sqns)
10 Portugal Cuirassiers (6 sqns)
11 Schmerzing Cuirassiers (6 sqns)
12 Saxon Graf Brühl Chevauxleger (4 sqns)
13 Saxon Prinz Karl Chevauxlegers (4 sqns)
14 Saxon Prinz Albrecht Chevauxleger (4 sqns)
15 Savoyen Dragoons (6 sqns)
16 Birkenfeld Cuirassiers (6 sqns)
17 Saxon Garde Carabiniers (2 sqns)

Right Wing
18 Salm-Salm IR (remnants of 2 bns)
19 Gaisruck IR (2 bns)
20 Neipperg IR (3 bns)
21 Kommandierten Cavalry (1,000 men)
22 Croats
23 Six battalions of Wied's command and Haller IR (2 bns) rallying

THE BATTLE OF KOLIN

18th June 1757, viewed from the south-east showing the ill-fated charge of Lieutenant-General Pennavaire's cavalry and the mauling of Lieutenant-General Tresckow's infantry.

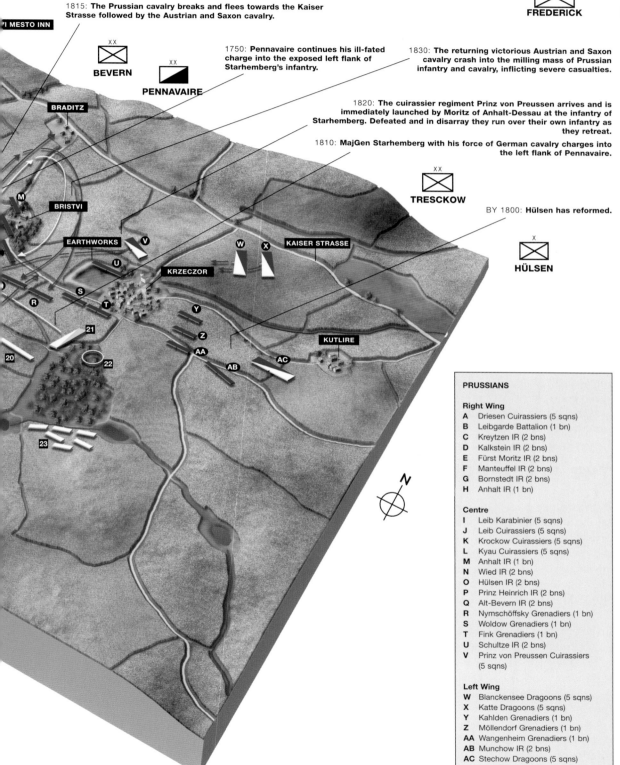

1815: The Prussian cavalry breaks and flees towards the Kaiser Strasse followed by the Austrian and Saxon cavalry.

VI MESTO INN

XX
BEVERN

XX
PENNAVAIRE

1750: Pennavaire continues his ill-fated charge into the exposed left flank of Starhemberg's infantry.

1830: The returning victorious Austrian and Saxon cavalry crash into the milling mass of Prussian infantry and cavalry, inflicting severe casualties.

XXXX
FREDERICK

BRADITZ

1820: The cuirassier regiment Prinz von Preussen arrives and is immediately launched by Moritz of Anhalt-Dessau at the infantry of Starhemberg. Defeated and in disarray they run over their own infantry as they retreat.

1810: MajGen Starhemberg with his force of German cavalry charges into the left flank of Pennavaire.

M

BRISTVI

XX
TRESCKOW

BY 1800: Hülsen has reformed.

EARTHWORKS

V

U

W   X

KAISER STRASSE

X
HÜLSEN

KRZECZOR

S

R

T

Y

21

Z

KUTLIRE

20

AA

22

AB

AC

23

N

PRUSSIANS

Right Wing
A   Driesen Cuirassiers (5 sqns)
B   Leibgarde Battalion (1 bn)
C   Kreytzen IR (2 bns)
D   Kalkstein IR (2 bns)
E   Fürst Moritz IR (2 bns)
F   Manteuffel IR (2 bns)
G   Bornstedt IR (2 bns)
H   Anhalt IR (1 bn)

Centre
I   Leib Karabinier (5 sqns)
J   Leib Cuirassiers (5 sqns)
K   Krockow Cuirassiers (5 sqns)
L   Kyau Cuirassiers (5 sqns)
M   Anhalt IR (1 bn)
N   Wied IR (2 bns)
O   Hülsen IR (2 bns)
P   Prinz Heinrich IR (2 bns)
Q   Alt-Bevern IR (2 bns)
R   Nymschöffsky Grenadiers (1 bn)
S   Woldow Grenadiers (1 bn)
T   Fink Grenadiers (1 bn)
U   Schultze IR (2 bns)
V   Prinz von Preussen Cuirassiers (5 sqns)

Left Wing
W   Blanckensee Dragoons (5 sqns)
X   Katte Dragoons (5 sqns)
Y   Kahlden Grenadiers (1 bn)
Z   Möllendorf Grenadiers (1 bn)
AA Wangenheim Grenadiers (1 bn)
AB Munchow IR (2 bns)
AC Stechow Dragoons (5 sqns)

retired in complete chaos, trampling over the supporting infantry behind. Tresckow's command was simultaneously assailed in their rear by Saxon and Austrian cavalrymen returning from routing Pennavaire's command. The Saxon's gave little quarter as they avenged the disaster of Hohenfriedberg in 1745. The two battalions of IR7 were broken, but not before the third rank of the regiment had tried, unsuccessfully, to about face and fire at the oncoming cavalry; the Nymschöfsky Grenadier Battalion (33/42) was cut down en masse. The final disaster for Tresckow came when he was wounded and taken prisoner. Exhaustion, dust and the smell of cordite swept over sunny Krzeczor Hill as early evening approached and both Daun and Frederick looked around for fresh troops to decide the contest.

Charge of an unknown regiment of Austrian dragoons. The only two regiments at Kolin with red coats and blue facings were Saxe-Gotha and Jüng-Modena, both were part of Stampach's abortive movement against Schonaich and were not as energetic! (Oil sketch by V. Blaas/HGM)

THE FINAL PRUSSIAN ATTACK

Both commanders cast their eyes towards Przerovsky Hill. Frederick broke off the attacks on Przerovsky Hill at about 6.00pm and at 6.30 the reinforced division of Andlau swept down the hill to retake Chotzemitz. Frederick in the meantime was moving all available forces to the left of his line to take advantage of the gap that still existed in the Austrian position on Krzeczor Hill. The regiments coming from his right wing were IR22 (Fürst Moritz), IR40 (Kreytzen), IR25 (Kalkstein) and the resilient Leibgarde battalion. They would join the remaining battalions of Tresckow and Hülsen. Frederick positioned himself near Bristvi to organise the infantry for the attack and then rode to bring up the 7th Cuirassier Regiment (Driesen) and to give orders for Major-General Normann with his two regiments from the right wing, 2nd (Blanckensee) and 4th (Katte) Dragoons, to support the centre. The 20 squadrons of Pennavaire's command were reorganised and formed part of the reserve.

Nor had Daun been idle. He too was ordering all available forces up to reinforce his right. The divisions of Puebla and Andlau were still on their way when at 7.00pm the shattered divisions of Sincere and Starhemberg had to face the next Prussian attack. The Prussian infantry

The First Battalion Leibgarde at the battle of Kolin fighting off the Hesse-Darmstadt Dragoons. (ASKB)

Field Marshal Daun in the centre urges his cavalry into action, possibly the Serbelloni Cuirassiers at the end of the battle (ASKB)

breasted the hill, pushing back the remnants of Salm-Salm, while the devastated regiments of Baden-Baden and Deutschmeister gave way completely. The resilience of Regiment Botta was once again going to be tested. They were still facing eastwards when Sincere galloped over to Andlau's Division and 'commandeered' the regiment Erzherzog Karl to extend the line to the south of Regiment Botta. This timely act enabled the Austrian line to meet the threat of the 14 Prussian battalions who were wheeling on IR40 to face the regiment of Botta. The Austrian line was still very short and the left flank was open to IR40 and while the regiments of Botta and Erzherzog Karl kept up a continuous fire on the Prussian line, Sincere gathered all the grenadiers he could and formed them into a battalion on the left of the regiment Botta. It was at this point that the Regiment Botta had again begun to run out of

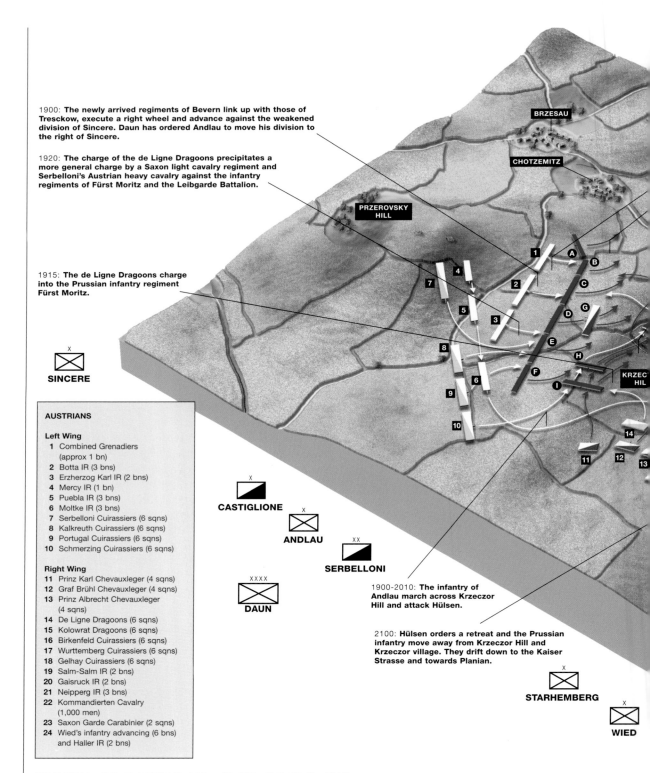

1900: The newly arrived regiments of Bevern link up with those of Tresckow, execute a right wheel and advance against the weakened division of Sincere. Daun has ordered Andlau to move his division to the right of Sincere.

1920: The charge of the de Ligne Dragoons precipitates a more general charge by a Saxon light cavalry regiment and Serbelloni's Austrian heavy cavalry against the infantry regiments of Fürst Moritz and the Leibgarde Battalion.

1915: The de Ligne Dragoons charge into the Prussian infantry regiment Fürst Moritz.

1900-2010: The infantry of Andlau march across Krzeczor Hill and attack Hülsen.

2100: Hülsen orders a retreat and the Prussian infantry move away from Krzeczor Hill and Krzeczor village. They drift down to the Kaiser Strasse and towards Planian.

BRZESAU

CHOTZEMITZ

PRZEROVSKY HILL

KRZEC HILL

SINCERE

CASTIGLIONE

ANDLAU

SERBELLONI

DAUN

STARHEMBERG

WIED

AUSTRIANS

Left Wing
1 Combined Grenadiers (approx 1 bn)
2 Botta IR (3 bns)
3 Erzherzog Karl IR (2 bns)
4 Mercy IR (1 bn)
5 Puebla IR (3 bns)
6 Moltke IR (3 bns)
7 Serbelloni Cuirassiers (6 sqns)
8 Kalkreuth Cuirassiers (6 sqns)
9 Portugal Cuirassiers (6 sqns)
10 Schmerzing Cuirassiers (6 sqns)

Right Wing
11 Prinz Karl Chevauxleger (4 sqns)
12 Graf Brühl Chevauxleger (4 sqns)
13 Prinz Albrecht Chevauxleger (4 sqns)
14 De Ligne Dragoons (6 sqns)
15 Kolowrat Dragoons (6 sqns)
16 Birkenfeld Cuirassiers (6 sqns)
17 Wurttemberg Cuirassiers (6 sqns)
18 Gelhay Cuirassiers (6 sqns)
19 Salm-Salm IR (2 bns)
20 Gaisruck IR (2 bns)
21 Neipperg IR (3 bns)
22 Kommandierten Cavalry (1,000 men)
23 Saxon Garde Carabinier (2 sqns)
24 Wied's infantry advancing (6 bns) and Haller IR (2 bns)

THE BATTLE OF KOLIN

18th June 1757, viewed from the south-east showing the final struggle for the Krzeczor Hill and the Prussian withdrawal.

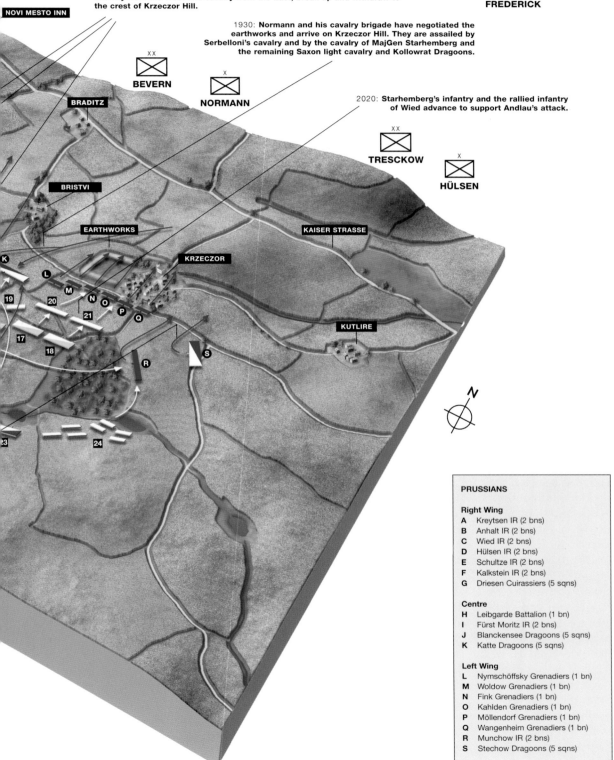

1945–2000: The Prussian infantry being simultaneously attacked by Austrian infantry from the West and cavalry from the East, break up and withdraw to the crest of Krzeczor Hill.

NOVI MESTO INN

1930: Normann and his cavalry brigade have negotiated the earthworks and arrive on Krzeczor Hill. They are assailed by Serbelloni's cavalry and by the cavalry of MajGen Starhemberg and the remaining Saxon light cavalry and Kollowrat Dragoons.

XXXX
FREDERICK

XX
BEVERN

X
NORMANN

2020: Starhemberg's infantry and the rallied infantry of Wied advance to support Andlau's attack.

XX
TRESCKOW

X
HÜLSEN

BRADITZ

BRISTVI

EARTHWORKS

KAISER STRASSE

KRZECZOR

K

L

M

N O P

19   Q

20   21

17

18   KUTLIRE

R   S

3

24

N

PRUSSIANS

Right Wing
A Kreytsen IR (2 bns)
B Anhalt IR (2 bns)
C Wied IR (2 bns)
D Hülsen IR (2 bns)
E Schultze IR (2 bns)
F Kalkstein IR (2 bns)
G Driesen Cuirassiers (5 sqns)

Centre
H Leibgarde Battalion (1 bn)
I Fürst Moritz IR (2 bns)
J Blanckensee Dragoons (5 sqns)
K Katte Dragoons (5 sqns)

Left Wing
L Nymschöffsky Grenadiers (1 bn)
M Woldow Grenadiers (1 bn)
N Fink Grenadiers (1 bn)
O Kahlden Grenadiers (1 bn)
P Möllendorf Grenadiers (1 bn)
Q Wangenheim Grenadiers (1 bn)
R Munchow IR (2 bns)
S Stechow Dragoons (5 sqns)

ammunition and their enterprising commander Colonel Prince Franz von Kinsky seized at pistol point an ammunition resupply intended for Regiment Moltke. Botta could now sustain another action, which was just as well as, with Andlau's Division still on their way, there were only four tired and depleted battalions and an ad hoc grenadier battalion to hold the Austrian line against 14 Prussian battalions. For a time Regiment Erzherzog Karl came close to being overwhelmed but with a fortitude which had been displayed throughout the day by their comrades in Regiment Botta, they held firm, firing low and only at point blank range.

Following behind the 14 battalions in the first Prussian line were the two battalions of IR22 and the Leibgarde Battalion and the 7th Cuirassiers. This breakthrough threatened the flank of the de Ligne and Kolowrat Dragoons, who were on the other side of the gap, and at this moment they received an order from Major-General Prince Lobkowitz to retire. Acting Major Schonnomyn responded that the de Ligne regiment had not come all the way from the Netherlands to do nothing. Legend also has it that the commanding officer Colonel de Thiennes asked Daun for permission to attack, and received his grudging assent with the comment: 'But you won't be able to do great things with your people – they haven't got moustaches!' De Thiennes turned and repeated this to his regiment and cried out: 'Boys, just show you can bite even if you haven't got any moustaches! Just show you need teeth to bite, and not whiskers!' This conversation is probably apocryphal as Daun was on the other side of the gap with Regiment Botta. A more likely candidate is the sarcastic Serbelloni for whom moustaches would have been an important status symbol of the soldier. Either way the dragoon regiments of de Ligne and Kolowrat, supported by those of Württemberg, the Kalkreuth Cuirassiers and the Saxon Chevauxleger Regiment Prinz Karl, wheeled left and charged towards the exposed Prussian infantry at the head of the breakthrough. The attack by Serbelloni's command precipitated the Schmerzing and Serbelloni Cuirassiers on the west side of the gap to join in the headlong rush to engage the enemy. The Prussian IR22 had advanced furthest over Krzeczor Hill and paid for their fortitude dearly. The regiment, which so far had seen very little action, suffered 77 per cent casualties – the fighting on the gentle southern slopes of Krzeczor Hill was a massacre. The Leibgarde Battalion once again had to about face their rear rank to fight off a cavalry attack and again they were ridden down, picked themselves up and marched away in proper order. Apart from the 7th Cuirassiers, who were supporting the 14 battalions of the main breakthrough, the only Prussian cavalry regiments to appear on the top of Krzeczor Hill were the Normann's 2nd and 4th Dragoons. By the time they had negotiated the passage between the 'Swedish Earthworks' and Bristvi, the Prussian position was in chaos on top of the hill. They stood no chance – their right flank was fired on by the Hungarian Regiment Erzherzog Karl, their left flank was engulfed by Major-General Starhemberg's Kommandierten cavalry and the Saxon regiments of Prinz Albert and Graf Brühl and they were overwhelmed by the swirling mass of cavalry from Serbelloni's command. This was too much and yet again the Prussian cavalry was swept from the ridge. The 14 battalions facing the regiments of Botta and Erzherzog Karl and the grenadiers now found themselves assailed in front by Andlau's Division supported by the Kalckreuth and Portugal Cuirassiers

Kolín, Kolíne! na póĺnej rovinĕ;
nejeden synáček u tebe zahyne.
Kolíne, Kolíne! nejsi hoden státi,
nejedna matička synáčka tam strati.
Matička synáčka, sestřička bratriĉka,
nejedna panenĉka svého milovniĉka.

**Kolin, Kolin! Set in a pretty lowland,
More than one son is going to die there.
Kolin, Kolin! It cannot be prevented,
More than one mother's son will be lost there.
One mother's little son, one sister's brother,
More than one maid her lover
(M. Ales/Author's collection)**

RIGHT **Looking north up the saddle between the Krzeczor Hill (R) and Przerovsky Hill (L). Daun's makeshift line to counter the 14 Prussian battalions is on the right of the picture. Infantry regiments Mercy and Puebla would have been marching from the vegetation on the left of the picture across our front (behind the tree in the foreground). (Author)**

BELOW **Saxon cavalry destroy Prussian infantry at Kolin at the climax of the battle. The infantryman in the foreground has lace on his coat indicating that he is a member of the Leibgarde battalion, who were ridden down for the second time at the end of the day, yet the survivors picked themselves up and marched away in true guardsman style with discipline restored. (Engraving after Menzel/PH)**

and in their rear by Serbelloni's cavalry. Between 7.30 and 8.00pm the Prussian line slowly broke up, the battalions falling back to form an irregular line on the crest of the hill. Here they made a last stand until their ammunition ran out, then making an about turn they marched off for the Kaiser Strasse in small groups, their muskets at the trail.

During the afternoon the indomitable Hülsen with the remnants of his seven battalions had retaken, and was still holding on to, the Oak Wood and remained in Krzeczor village as well. He now faced the last threat of his long day as the regiments of Puebla and Moltke and a battalion of Mercy made their way across the casualty strewn reverse slope of Krzeczor Hill from the west and the battalions of Wied's Division, now rallied, approached from the south. Hülsen continued to give a good account of

77

Frederick leaves the field with an escort of Garde du Corps. Frederick left the fields of Mollwitz and Lobositz early, thinking all was lost, only for his infantry to save the day. This was not to be the case at Kolin. Frederick had been defeated – the invincible aura was for ever tarnished. (Adam Hook)

himself until he too realised that the day was lost and at 9.00pm ordered the retreat. Like other infantrymen Hülsen's battalions withdrew in small groups towards the Kaiser Strasse, where Hülsen and Bevern did their best to direct the demoralised infantry along the Kaiser Strasse to Planian and safety. Zieten, who thought the battle had been going according to plan, received his orders to withdraw with disbelief.

Frederick, reminiscent of Mollwitz and Lobositz, left the field earlier than his army. On this occasion, however, there was to be no miraculous victory with his infantry winning the day. He arrived in Nimburg with his escort of Garde du Corps and hussars and the dejected King climbed to the ground and sat on a water pipe, drawing figures in the dust with his stick. As the Prussian train marched past a wounded cuirassier disturbed Frederick's thoughts with a drink of water in his hat. Frederick left Prince Moritz of Anhalt-Dessau to command the army and set off for Prague on 19 June.

Although Daun had Nadasty's hussar squadrons at his disposal neither Daun nor Nadasty issued orders to turn the Prussian retreat into a rout. Stampach on the far left could quite easily have disrupted the Prussian withdrawal along the Kaiser Strasse with the six totally fresh cavalry regiments of his command. However, in keeping with his overall performance during the battle he too issued no orders. For the Austrians the unthinkable had happened, after years of defeat they had finally beaten the Prussian King in open battle. It is, therefore, to an extent not surprising no further orders were issued, Daun and his commanders were totally unprepared for this even-tuality. On 19 June Nadasty took the light troops off in pursuit of the Prussians and the main army evacuated the stricken fields of the Krzeczor Hill and Przerovsky Hill and on 20 June the 'Te Deum' was sung after which in the evening a salute of a triple discharge of 100 pieces of cannon and all the muskets was fired.

The defeated Prussian King ponders his misfortune as he draws in the dust with his stick. (Engraving after Menzel/PH)

On the evening of the battle Lieutenant-Colonel Freiherr von Wetter was sent with the news of the victory to Vienna, where he arrived on 20 June, the day Frederick was raising the siege of Prague. Maria Theresa proclaimed the institution of the Military Order of Maria Theresa and the golden day of Kolin was designated as the birthday of the new order. Marshall Daun was nominated as the Order's Commander and received the Grand Cross of the Order. His son received a map of Bohemia on which Maria Theresa had inscribed in her own hand in gold lettering the name of the battle.

THE PRUSSIAN WITHDRAWAL FROM BOHEMIA

Frederick left the task of gathering his battered army at Nimburg to Moritz of Anhalt-Dessau and Bevern, while on 19 June he hastened back to Prague. On 20 June the siege of Prague was lifted and on the same day Frederick marched with the siege army to Lissa. Keith was entrusted with the siege train and ordered to withdraw to Leitmeritz via Budin, where Frederick would join him at a later date. Apart from the Austrians in Prague sallying out, falling upon Keith and inflicting severe losses, the raising of the siege went well. Far more could have been done by the Austrians in Prague to frustrate the Prussian moves, but Prince Charles of Lorraine was not the man to take his chances. Frederick arrived in Lissa on the 21 June to face the realities of his next move. He decided to adopt a 'wait and see' policy. Although he lost at Kolin and had been frustrated at the siege of Prague, he continued to find it difficult to credit the Austrians with any ability to seize the initiative, particularly as he still held the majority of ground he had gained in northern Bohemia. By holding on to his position he expected to frustrate the Austrians by keeping the war south of the border with Saxony, using up the supplies and fodder that might otherwise be used by his enemies in a counter-offensive. On 20 June while he was planning the next stages of his campaign, the victors of Kolin sang the 'Te Deum' and to the great misfortune of Austria, Prince Charles having recovered his health, assumed command of all Austrian forces in the theatre of operations.

A contemporary map showing the post-battle manoeuvres of each army. The most accurate is position 'F' with the Prussians around Nimburg. (MSW)

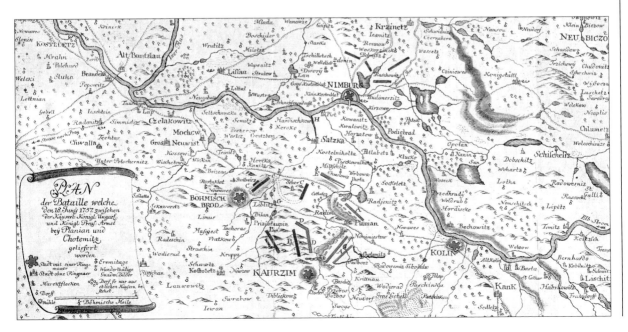

Bautzen

Wiessenberg

13

Görlitz

12

xxxx
**FREDERICK
(50,600)**

10

DRESDEN

Löbau

14

Neustadt

10

15

Ostritz

Pirna

River Elbe

9

Rumberg

14

Zittau

Kreywitz

9

13

Reichenberg

Kamnitz

Liebenau

xxx
**AUGUST WILLIAM
(30,800)**

Reichstadt

x
**PUTTKAMER
(1,954)**

Gabel

Bohm Leipa

xxxx
**PRINCE CHARLES
OF LORRAINE
(70–100,000)**

8

Niemes

River Iser

Neuschloss

11

Aussig

12

Hühnenwasser

Swigan

xxxx
**FREDERICK
(34,000)**

xx
WIED

7a

10

Leitmeritz

7

9

Münchengrätz

Lobositz

5

River Elbe

River Iser

8

Jung-Bunzlau

River Eger

Budin

4

Melnik

xxx
**AUGUST WILLIAM
(33,800)**

River Moldau

7a

xx
NADASTI

7

6

Alt-Lissa

5

Alt-Bunzlau

Brandeis

Lissa

Czelakowitz

3

6b

Nimberg

4

2

6

6a

Poczemitz

xxxxx
**PRINCE CHARLES/
DAUN
(70,000)**

2

PRAGUE

5

1

Skworetz

Planian

Schwartz
Koseletz

Kaurzim

4

3

1

Kolin

xxxx
DAUN

N

| 0 | | 10 miles |
| 0 | | 16 km |

PRUSSIAN MOVEMENTS
1. 18 June: Prussian army withdraws to Nimberg during the evening and night.
2. 19 June: Frederick goes to Prague in the early hours and raises the siege on the same day.
3. 20 June: Marches with the siege army to Lissa and arrives on 21 June.
4. 20 June: Keith with the siege train marches via Budin to Leitmeritz and arrives on 28 June.
5. Frederick sets off for Leitmeritz via Melnik to join Keith. Arrives on 27 June.
6. 30 June–3 July: Prince August William is in command at Jung-Bunzlau.
7. 3 July–7 July: Prussians march to Neuschloss.
7a. Puttkamer is detached to collect stores from Gabel. Captured in Gabel on 15 July.
8. 7 July: August William moves to Bohm Leipa and remains there until 16 July.
9. 16 July: The Prussians start their march to Zittau via Kamnitz, Kreywitz and Rumberg. They arrive on 22 July to find the Austrians have got there first. Make camp on the heights opposite the Eckartsberg.
10. 24 July: Unable to dislodge the Austrians August William strikes camp and marches to Lobau and then Bautzen. Ariives in Bautzen on 27 July.
11. 22 July: Frederick leaves Leitmeritz and marches, via Bautzen, to join August William at Zittau.
12. 29 July: Approaching from Dresden Frederick arrives in Bautzen.
13. 16 August: Frederick detaches five battalions to Görlitz.
14. 16 August: Frederick marches to Zittau.
15. After a few days near Zittau Frederick withdraws to Bautzen.

AUSTRIAN MOVEMENTS
1. 19–20 June: Daun remains in the area of the battle, singing a 'Te Deum' and firing a salute.
2. 19 June: Nadasti with light troops begins the pursuit of the Prussians. Remains south of the River Elbe.
3. 22 June: The Austrians march to Schwartz Koseletz.
4. 24 June: Daun marches to Skworetz.
5. 26 June: Austrians move to Ober-Poczemitz.
6. 29 June: Prince Charles of Lorraine arrives in Czelakowitz.
6a. 29 June: Daun arrives.
6b. 26 June: Nadasty arrives in Czelakowitz.
7. 1 July: The Austrians cross the River Elbe at Brandeis.
7a. 2 July: Nadasty detached to Melnik to watch Frederick.

8. 3 July: Austrians arrive at Jung-Bunzlau.
9. 3 July: Austrians push on to Münchengrätz and arrive on 7 July. Advance to Swigan on 8 July; back in Münchengrätz on 11 July.
10. 13 July: Main army marches to Hühnenwasser.
11. 12 July: Prince Charles arrives at Niemes.
12. Wied follows up the Prussians by advancing to Bohm Leipa and Reichstadt.
13. 15 July: Gabel is captured along with its stores and Puttkamer with his provision train.
14. Austrians arrive at Zittau and make camp on the Eckartsberg, north of Zittau.

ABOVE LEFT **Decoration worn around the neck of the Military Order of Maria Theresa. The Battle of Kolin was designated as the anniversary of the order and Marshal Daun was the first commander. (PH)**

ABOVE CENTRE **Breast star of the Military Order of Maria Theresa. (PH)**

ABOVE RIGHT **The Prussian Order of the Black Eagle. The breast star, bottom, and decoration worn around the neck, top. (Authors collection)**

The Austrian army under Daun rested on 21 June before moving in four columns to Schwartz Koseletz on 22 June. Frederick in the meantime had decided on his course of action, grateful for the usual lethargy that had once again beset the Austrians, he decided to take the bold step of dividing his army. He would take personal command of 34,000 men and would draw their supplies from the magazine at Leitmeritz; the remaining 33,800 would be entrusted to his brother, Prince August Wilhelm, who would draw on the magazine at Zittau, some 74km (44 English miles) as the crow flies to the north. With his plans made Frederick set off for Leitmeritz, and travelling via Melnik he arrived on 27 June. A day later Keith marched in with the siege train.

On 23 June at Schwartz Koseletz Daun learnt from Nadasty that the Prussians were at Nimburg. The next day Daun marched his army to Skworetz, where it encamped in three lines around the town. The Austrian army spent 24 June resting. Also on 24 June Prince Charles in Prague received word from Colonel Loudon, who was on the coat tails of Keith, that Keith was in the area of Lobositz and in order to make his position more secure Keith had broken up the road and made obstacles to movement in the countryside. On 25 June Daun went to Prague to pay his respects to Prince Charles and to discuss with him the course of action they should take. Regrettably for the Austrians the one man bold enough to give strong leadership lay dying and on the morning of 26 June Field Marshal Browne passed away. In the meanwhile Daun and Prince Charles had decided to remain in the vicinity of Prague until they received the tents that had been made for them in Moravia. Until these arrived the soldiers who lost their tents at the Battle of Prague would have to make do with leaves or bark! On 26 June Daun moved his command to Ober-Poczemitz and Nadasty set up his headquarters at Czelakowitz. The concentration of the two armies was finally achieved on 29 June, some 11 days after Kolin, when Daun and Prince Charles arrived at Czelakowitz.

While in Leitmeritz Frederick received the news that his mother, Queen Sophia Dorothea, had died on 28 June. This was a terrible blow to Frederick, who had always been very close to his mother. It appears that while August Wilhelm had been left with the unenviable task of operating north of the Elbe on an axis Nimburg-Zittau and against a far more numerous enemy, Frederick withdrew into himself and sorrowed at his misfortune. Prince August Wilhelm with his advisors, Winterfeld, Zieten and Schmettau, decided to shorten his lines of communication with Zittau and put some distance between himself and the newly combined Austrian army. On 30 June he moved his force to Jung-Bunzlau, where they remained until 3 July. On 1 July August Wilhelm's patrols told him that the combined Austrian army was on the move and had crossed the Elbe at Brandeis and were continuing their march to Jung-Bunzlau. With their respective cavalry patrols observing each other and Nadasty with his Croats closing in fast on August Wilhelm, he decided to move to Neuschloss on the morning of 3 July. At the same time it was decided to send Puttkamer with 3,000 men to collect stores from Gabel. The Prussians had barely marched off when during the afternoon the lead elements of the Austrians arrived in Jung-Bunzlau.

Although on 2 July Nadasty had been sent to Melnik to watch Frederick with an extra five battalions, ten companies of grenadiers and two cavalry regiments, it was becoming clear to August Wilhelm, if not to Frederick, that the Austrians were directing their efforts against him and not the King. Neuschloss was considered a good position and with command of the local area it would have proved difficult for the Austrians to dislodge the Prussians, particularly as they had the advantage of being closer to Frederick at Leitmeritz, who would almost certainly reinforce August Wilhelm if the need arose. There was a lot of unease in the Prussian camp and August Wilhelm remained at Neuschloss until 7 July before once again retiring, this time to Bohm Leipa on the advice of Winterfeld. August Wilhelm stayed in Bohm Leipa for nine days. During this time there was a lengthy correspondence with Frederick, from whom August Wilhelm was looking for advice about his courses for withdrawal or otherwise, this was not forthcoming except the comment that 'when you get to Berlin you will have to halt!'

There is no doubt that one of the root causes of the continued withdrawal by August Wilhelm was the increasingly effective work being done by the Croats of Beck and Morocz, who were in the Prussians rear area as well as perpetually snapping away at the Prussian coat tails and morale. The other problem for August Wilhelm was that Daun and Prince Charles were controlling events, with the Prussians having to react to the movements of the Austrians. The main Austrian army having marched to Swigan on 8 July was back in

Marshal Daun with his victorious Austrian army relieves Prague after Kolin. (Author's collection)

Crown Prince August Wilhelm (1722–1758) by Antoine Pense, in the uniform of IR18 (Prinz von Preussen) of which he was Colonel. August Wilhelm was not as competent in the field as his two brothers, King Frederick II and Prince Henry, he was however a brave and loyal man who was put in command of the eastern part of the army after Kolin. The demoralised Prussians were pushed out of Bohemia in disarray into Lusatia as the Austrians outmanoeuvred Augustus Wilhelm and captured the magazine of Zittau. Frederick, when they next met, publicly humiliated his brother for his mishandling of his command and dismissed him from military service. He died a year later. Frederick's wrath was almost certainly the result of knowing that instead of skulking at Leitmeritz feeling sorry for himself, he should have been in command in the area of most danger to his forces after Kolin. (PM)

Münchengrätz on 11 July after indecision on the part of Daun and Prince Charles. On 13 July the army marched to Hühnenwasser, at the same time detaching the corps of Wied to Reichstadt and those of Macquire and Arenberg to invest Gabel. On the evening of 14 July in Bohm Leipa, cannon fire was heard coming from the north-east. Hussars soon confirmed the bad news that Gabel was under attack by regular troops and that Puttkammer was defending vigorously and expecting to be relieved within a few hours. Some hard decisions needed to be made and August Wilhelm called a Council of War. The most sensible of his advisors, Winterfeld, had retired to bed, tired after a day in the saddle, and did not attend. August Wilhelm was faced with three choices – firstly he could withdraw to Frederick at Leitmeritz, thereby giving up Zittau as well. This course of action would almost certainly bring the Royal wrath upon his head. Secondly he could retire safely through the hills via Kamnitz and Rumberg to Zittau. These first two options of necessity required abandoning Puttkamer to his fate in Gabel. The third option was to march to the aid of Puttkammer, informing Frederick of his actions, engage the Austrians and dispute Gabel to the last and if necessary withdraw to Zittau. For some time August Wilhelm was convinced that this third option was the best course of action, crying out that with 30,000 Prussians and only 24km to Gabel, the objective could be achieved. The Counsellors seeing 24km to Gabel and 24 more to Zittau, through difficult terrain with their right flank exposed to the Austrians, were against this course of action and in the end they sowed the seeds of doubt in August Wilhelm's mind. Fearing Frederick's wrath and possible failure at Gabel the worst course of action was chosen. August Wilhelm decided to skulk around the western flank and marching nearly twice the distance try to beat the Austrians to Zittau, hoping that way at least to achieve something. The Prussians struck camp on 16 July and with the Croats still sniping at their heels, made their way via Kamnitz, Kreywitz and Rumberg, arriving outside Zittau on 22 July only to find to their horror that the Austrians had beaten them and were encamped to the north of Zittau on the Eckartsberg, which commands the town. Prince August Wilhelm did send eight battalions to assist Puttkammer in Gabel on 16 July but they found their way blocked and had to retrace their steps. On 15 July Puttkammer had asked for terms; with four battalions, a squadron of hussars, eight cannon and numerous wagons and horses – in total 1,954 men – the Prussians marched into captivity and the Austrians occupied Gabel. The Austrians now had only a short march to Zittau, which they carried out in stages. The Left Wing of the army arriving on 20 July and the Right Wing on 21 July.

Frederick on hearing about the loss of Gabel was convinced that his presence was needed with August Wilhelm in Saxony. On 21 July, leaving Keith to bring the Royal army out of Bohemia, Frederick left Leitmeritz and set out for Zittau. Unable to dislodge the Austrians from their positions, August Wilhelm struck his camp on 24 July and withdrew to Bautzen, arriving on 27 July. It was here that Frederick met up with him a few days later on 29 July. The next day Frederick interviewed his tired and demoralised brother. The Royal anger was such that August Wilhelm left the meeting in tears. Frederick compounded the humiliation with a letter, saying that never again would his brother be given an army to ruin. August Wilhelm retired from the army and within a year was dead from a cerebral haemorrhage.

A painting in the Kolin Regional Museum of Prince Charles of Lorraine being invested with the Military Order of Maria Theresa. (Author's collection)

Frederick was determined in this high summer to deal with the Austrians. The Prussian army with Frederick at Bautzen comprised 50,600 men and 72 cannon. The Austrians on the other hand had gathered all their forces and an army of 100,000 now stood at Zittau. On 16 August Frederick detached five battalions to Görlitz with the intention of delaying and warning him of any Austrian flank march. The main army marched to Zittau and arrived there on the same day with the Austrians on the Eckartsberg watching Frederick ride through his position, issuing orders. The lessons of Prague and Kolin should have made him cautious of attacking the Austrians on ground of their choosing, but Frederick was determined to attack the right flank of the Austrian position. Prince Henry on the other hand was convinced that such an attack would destroy the Prussian army and in the evening went to his brother's headquarters at Tittelsdorf. Here he found Frederick at supper under a tree, surrounded by a few of his generals. He was telling them of how he would beat the Austrians the next day and describing all sorts of incredible plans. Prince Henry spoke to his brother and they entered Frederick's quarters and as the generals gathered outside in a gentle, but warm rain, the two brothers were clearly having an animated discussion that went on for the best part of 1½ hours. In the end Prince Henry came out to announce that the next day would be a rest day. The army was overjoyed and was eternally grateful to the Prince for preventing what they saw as their demise the next day. The generals also saw in him a restraining influence on their seemingly ever more aggressive King. The Prussians withdrew towards their magazine at Bautzen on 20 August and brought to an end the first campaign of 1757.

FREDERICK'S DEFEAT AND THE PRINCIPLES OF WAR

After Kolin Frederick laid the blame for the defeat at the tactical level on Manstein, whom he held responsible for the all-out attacks on Chotzemitz and Przerovsky Hill. The British envoy, Mitchell, has given us the best reason when he stated 'The cause of our misfortune is chiefly owing to the great success the King of Prussia's arms have had in eight successive battles against the Austrians; and particularly to the victory he obtained near Prague, on the 6th of May, which has made His Prussian Majesty imagine that he could force them from the most advantageous posts.' It is highly unlikely that the term 'Principles of War' was in Frederick's vocabulary as it is a modern term, bringing together the thoughts and writings of military strategists and theorists since his time. Frederick was, however, a great writer and it is in *The King of Prussia's Military Instructions to his Generals* that we find his 'maxims' (Principles of War) on conducting operations in the eighteenth century.

It is worth examining the Principles of war in relation to Frederick's defeat at Kolin. Failure in a campaign or defeat in a battle are a far better illustration of the Principles than victory, when their normally correct application has led to success. In any campaign or engagement the **selection and maintenance of the aim** is one of the commander's most important tasks, requiring clear and logical thought. The selection of the aim is also dependent on the information available to the commander about the enemy's forces and dispositions as a result of reconnaissance. Having selected his aim the commander must make sure it is

Frederick and Zieten on a reconnaissance during the Seven Years War. (Print after Richard Knotel)

unambiguous and can be achieved with the forces available to him. The aim must then be disseminated as far down as possible to allow commanders at all levels to understand what the commander is trying to achieve so that their efforts will help fulfil the aim. It is clear that Frederick having decided to attack Daun had selected his aim. However, we must question if he really did have the forces available with him to achieve his aim of turning Daun's right flank and rolling up his position on Przerovsky Hill and Krezczor Hill. In addition, was he correct in selecting this aim, particularly as a proper reconnaissance of the Austrian positions had not been done? The details of the plan had certainly reached the 'brigade' commanders, but one doubts if it went any lower, particularly when the plan of attack changed.

Another important principle a commander must consider is that of **morale**. Napoleon's dictum, 'Morale is to material as three is to one', shows the value he placed on this invisible asset. High morale gives a soldier the confidence required to carry out the commander's wishes and win the battle. A good commander will always look to the well being of his men and this means being sensitive to the stresses and strains incurred by the soldiers who do the dirty work at the tactical level. This does not mean a commander becomes a social worker, but in this case Frederick's army had fought an exceptionally difficult battle six weeks earlier at Prague and the casualties had been the highest suffered by the Prussians in any battle to date. 'These are no longer the old Austrians', was a remark by a Prussian soldier after Lobositz in 1756 and this had been borne out at Prague. It would be wrong to say morale was low in the Prussian army, but the rank and file and the junior officers were only too aware that the Austrians were proving themselves difficult to beat on ground of their own choosing as at Prague. The Austrians had once again chosen their ground and if there was to be a battle, the Prussian army would be required to attack. We must also not forget that at Prague both sides had been of an equal size – this would not be the case at Kolin.

The only principle that Frederick was giving serious consideration before Kolin was **offensive action**. Offensive action is a commander's means of influencing the outcome of a battle or campaign. By adopting offensive action Frederick was taking the initiative, thereby giving himself the ability to take the action necessary to secure a decision. The benefits for morale that offensive action brings in creating confidence and an ascendency over the enemy cannot be underestimated but they can be wiped out by a commander believing that he can attack the enemy indiscriminately and regardless of casualties.

For his plan to attack Daun to be a success Frederick needed **surprise** on his side. Bearing in mind that Daun occupied the high ground and was able to follow Frederick's movements with ease, Frederick was totally unable to satisfy the elements required for surprise – secrecy, deception, originality, audacity and speed. The only element Frederick came close to satisfying was audacity. He was lamentably inept at providing the others. Secrecy and deception would always be difficult at Kolin, but by attempting to turn the Austrian right flank, something he had done at Prague, he was not being original and with nearly 20km to march just to get into a position to attack Daun, speed would be at a premium and if he did force march his army for too long they would be in no fit state to carry out his plan.

On most occasions military success is dependent on the result of the **concentration of force**, a superior force, at a given time and place. In most cases for the attacker to be successful he will need to outnumber the enemy, ideally, by three to one. Frederick was planning to attack Daun, yet his infantry who would be required to attack and hold the ground numbered only 19,500 compared to Daun who had 34,000; a difference of 14,500 men. He was almost equal in cavalry but was woefully short in artillery. Indeed the Austrian infantry alone equalled in numbers his entire army.

The situation demanded that Frederick apply a proper **economy of effort**. It was impossible for Frederick to be strong everywhere and in order to mass a decisive strength at a critical time and place he could not afford for wasteful dispersal of his resources. Frederick wasted his infantry resources by allowing the attacks to continue on Przerovsky Hill, when it was clear that the mass would be required on Krzeczor Hill to push home any advantage gained by Hülsen. It was late in the day when he realised that Kreczor Hill was the place where the battle would be won or lost. By then it was too late, his cavalry had been repulsed three times, the infantry of Hulsen, Tresckow and Manstein were exhausted and they still made up the majority of his mass. His final attack was in the balance before it even got under way.

As General Field Marshal Graf von Moltke famously said, 'No plan of operations can look with any certainty beyond the first meeting with the major forces of the enemy.' As such any commander must allow for **flexibility**. Frederick demonstrates time and again his incredible ability to be flexible. Kolin is again an example of this: when he realises that the village of Krzeczor is occupied, he adjusts his plan of attack accordingly. The problem for Frederick was that it was too late; his flexibility could not rescue a fundamentally flawed plan.

As the army streams away from Kolin, a wounded trooper of the 11th Cuirassiers offers his dejected king a drink of water with the words, 'Drink your majesty, and let battles be battles; it's well that you are safe. Let us trust in God that it will soon be our turn to conquer!' (Print after Richard Knotel)

Kolin however does illustrate that the Prussian infantry were a highly disciplined and motivated force for them to accomplish what they did. The cavalry on the other hand had a mixed day. Krosigk's charge was devastating and gave Frederick his best chance of winning the battle. The cavalry of Pennavaire, Schonaich and Normann were not handled well. The young Colonel Seyditz was awarded the *Pour le Merite* and promoted out of turn to Major-General with the task of regenerating the Prussian cavalry. Despite his failure to apply the principles we have discussed, his dogged infantry almost won the day for Frederick at Kolin and in so doing, as they had done before, reinforced his belief that he really could defeat the Austrians where and when he wished.

THE BATTLEFIELD AND KOLIN TODAY

I visited the battlefield of Kolin with my eldest son, Rupert, in May/June 2000 and we were lucky enough for the weather to be sunny and warm, the same sort of weather as the Prussians and Austrians had all those years ago. If you wish to make the visit yourself the map you will need is the *Edice Klubu Ceskych Turisu No.42, KOLINSKO A KUTNOHOROSKO, Turistická Mapa (Hiking Map),* 1:50,000, (ISBN 80-85499-83-5), I purchased mine in the UK from The Map Shop in Upton-on-Severn (01684 – 593146). I was subsequently told that the map is out of print, but they were available to buy in the Czech Republic.

The battlefield, as battlefields go, is remarkably unspoilt. The only major changes to the scenery are the village of Kamhajek, north of Krzeczor, which did not exist in 1757, the slight enlargement of the villages, except for Bristvi, which is pretty much the same size, and the communications tower, which is being erected slap bang in the middle, just as Przerovsky Hill rises out of the saddle with Krzeczor Hill and 700m south of Chotzemitz. Some of the roads are now metalled, which they were not in 1757. This part of Bohemia has always been a farm in the greater sense, with a rich carpet of fields spreading as far as the eye can see. Cereal crops are still grown on the site of the battlefield today. An additional crop is the small vineyard just below the monument. The 'Zlate Slunce' (Golden Sun) Inn on the Kaiser Strasse today is not the same as the inn of three storeys mentioned in so many texts. There was an inn on the same site in 1757, but this was called the 'U slunce' (At the Sun) in the hamlet of Braditz. Frederick never visited this inn. The inn he did visit was called 'Novi Mesto' (New Town) and was situated 2km west of the 'U slunce' and has subsequently been destroyed. He is said to have gone to the first floor of the inn, which would make sense as the majority of country buildings in Bohemia at the time were single storey, an inn with a first floor was a substantial building.

The ground rolls and rises gently from the Kaiser Strasse towards the hills, with the villages of Brzesau and Chotzemitz nestling into the landscape. Of the two hills, Przerovsky Hill has the steepest approach, although overall the ground is

The monument of the Imperial double headed eagle stands at the north-western corner of the earthworks. Erected in 1898 it unashamedly celebrates Maria Theresa's first victory over Frederick the Great. (Author)

RIGHT **The centre of Krzeczor village today, which remains substantially unchanged from the time of the battle. The buildings are more modern that those of 1757, but you do get a good feel for how the village looked at the time. (Author)**

RIGHT **The author is standing in the area of the Oak Wood. The cherry trees and bushes mark the northern tip of the old Oak Wood, which no longer exists. Modern houses of Krzeczor can be seen in the distance. (Author)**

BELOW **A small religious shrine on the road from Brzesau to Chotzemitz. Przerovsky Hill can be seen in the background. Prussian IR40, 25 and 22 were in this area before moving to Frederick's left flank for the final Prussian attack. (Author)**

not difficult. The gully cutting into Przerovsky Hill, the ravine at Bristvi and the valley to the north east of Krzeczor are quite deep and would have caused problems for the Prussian attacks. All the hills are convex in cross-section and so in order for Daun to easily observe what Frederick was up to he must have deployed his battalions on the forward slope. The reverse of the position shows quite clearly how easy it was for Daun to move his reserves from point A to point B unobserved by Frederick. The cereal crops grow across the top of both hills and terrain is almost like the steppes in its openness. When standing on the high points of the hills, due to the

The battlescene on the memorial commemorating the charge of the Austrian de Ligne Dragoons. (Author)

The armorial on the reverse of the monument commemorates the achievements of IR Botta and IR Deutschmeister. (Author)

convex slopes the Kaiser Strasse is in dead ground as is the village of Chotzemitz and Brzesau is just visible. Krzeczor is identifiable by the church spire. The Oak Wood has gone, it was a cabbage field when I visited. There is a scattering of small woods and it is impossible to be sure if they were standing on the day of the battle. They are however on the steepest parts of any slope and so I am fairly sure that there were trees in the same spot in 1757. There are also low bushes and scrubby hedges lining the road. These I suspect have grown up since the battle, but am sure similar vegetation was present in 1757. Like so many European villages, farms are an integral part of the village and help make them more substantial. Krzeczor of all the villages has grown in size, southwards and eastwards. The earthworks are still impressive nearly 370 years after their construction. They would certainly hinder any advance. In 1898 the Austrians erected an enormous monument to their victory at Kolin and it is situated on the north-west tip of the earthworks. It is well worth visiting and a splendid spot for a picnic. The openness of the battlefield allows one to follow easily the course of events.

The town of Kolin is not the most beautiful as a result of industrial plants and the decay of old buildings that was endemic in Eastern Bloc countries. Happily though the medieval core of Kolin has been preserved. Kolin was founded by German colonists in the 1250s. The streets are laid out in a chess board fashion and the main cobbled square, 'Karlovo náměstí', is easy to find. The Gothic church of St. Bartholomew, begun in 1261, stands on raised ground in the south-east corner of the old

Kolin town square. Kolin has its fair share of beautiful old buildings. Many however need serious repair work after years of neglect under the Communist regimes. (Author)

town. The modern stained glass window fills the interior with an intense blue light that disturbs the otherwise determinedly medieval atmosphere. Kolin also had a significant Jewish population which peaked at about 1,700 in the 1850s and has its tales of the Holocaust that wiped out the majority of the population. The Jewish ghetto was in the south-west corner of the old town, dominated by St. Bartholomew's, and even today has a run-down feel to it. The Regional Museum Kolin is opposite St. Bartholomew's church and you must ring the bell to be admitted. If you are in search of the history of Kolin, although small the museum has some very interesting artefacts. The Battle of Kolin has a small gallery dedicated to it. There is a stylised flat figure diorama of the battle and a small collection of weaponry. The most interesting feature is the original oil painting of Prince Charles of Lorraine being invested with the Military Order of Maria Theresa.

BIBLIOGRAPHY

General accounts:

Anderson, M.S., *Europe in the Eighteenth Century 1713–1783*, London (1961)

Atkinson, C.T., *A History of Germany 1715–1815*, London (1908)

Belina, P. *Kolin 18.6.1757*, Prague (1997)

Carlyle, T., *History of Friedrich II of Prussia, called Frederick the Great*, 8 volumes, London (1898)

Cogswell, N., *1757 The Defence of Prague, The Journal of Horace St.Paul from 7th May to 28th June including the Campaign of Marshal Daun*, Guisborough (1998)

Duffy, C., *Frederick the Great. A Military Life*, London (1985)

Duffy, C., *The Military Experience in the Age of Reason*, London (1987)

Engelmann, J. and Dorn, G., *Die Schlachten Friedrich des Grossen*, Utting (2001 rep)

Fraser, D., *Frederick the Great, King of Prussia*, London (2000)

Gödölley, J., *Military Historical Memorial, Vol 3*, Prague (1934)

Goslich, D., *Die Schlact bei Kolin 18 June 1757*, Berlin (1911)

Grossen Generalstabe, *Die Kriege Friedrichs des Grossen. Dritte Teil. Der siebenjahrige Krieg, 175– 1763, Vol. 3 Kolin*, 9 volumes, Berlin (1890–1910)

Hayes, C (trans.), *Frederick the Great's Instructions to his Generals*, Partizan Press, Leigh-on-Sea (1990)

Luvaas, J., *Frederick the Great on The Art of War*, New York (1999 rep)

Mitchell, A., *Memoirs and Papers of Sir Andrew Mitchell K.B.,* 2 vols, London (1850)

Prittwitz und Gaffron, C.W., *Unter der Fahne des Herzogs von Bevern*, Berlin (1935)

Schieder, T., *Frederick the Great*, London (2000)

Schmerfeld, v. F (ed), *General Field Marshal Graf von Moltke*, Berlin (1925)

For coverage of the two armies:

Duffy, C., *The Army of Frederick the Great*, Newton Abbot (1974)

Duffy, C., *The Army of Maria Theresa*, Doncaster (1990 rep)

Haythornthwaite, P.J., *Frederick the Great's Army: 1 Cavalry*, Men-at-Arms series 236, London (1991)

Haythornthwaite, P.J., *Frederick the Great's Army: 2 Infantry*, Men-at-Arms series 240, London (1991)

Haythornthwaite, P.J., *Frederick the Great's Army: 3 Specialist Troops*, Men-at-Arms series 248, London (1992)

Haythornthwaite, P.J., *The Austrian Army 1740-80: 1 Cavalry*, Men-at-Arms series 271, London (1994)

Haythornthwaite, P.J., *The Austrian Army 1740-80: 2 Infantry*, Men-at-Arms series 276, London (1994)

Haythornthwaite, P.J., *The Austrian Army 1740-80: 3 Specialist Troops*, Men-at-Arms series 280, London (1995)

INDEX

References to illustrations are shown in **bold**.